SO YOU WANT TO LEARN ABOUT
PITCHING

A Guide for Players, Parents, and Coaches

John Petre PhD

RoseDog Books
PITTSBURGH, PENNSYLVANIA 15238

RoseDog Books
585 Alpha Drive
Suite 103
Pittsburgh, PA 15238
Visit our website at *www.rosedogbookstore.com*

ISBN: 978-1-63867-840-3
eISBN: 978-1-63867-785-7

TABLE OF CONTENTS

Chapter I:

Introduction

Baseball is a very popular sport and one of the most important positions in baseball is the pitcher. The pitcher controls the game since they initiate the start of every play. They participate directly or indirectly in almost every active component of the game. The pitcher is clearly the most important player on the field of play and their skill level often dictates the result of the game. To that end, how does one become a pitcher? It seems like the importance of the position would have tremendous requirements for optimal performance. There is a lot of knowledge, skill and physical ability required to be a quality pitcher. Where can one find the information to learn or teach pitching? Where is there information to learn, practice and improve all aspects of pitching?

This book will present a vast collection of knowledge gathered over thirty years of teaching the art of pitching to youth of all ages. If you are a novice pitcher, or an experienced high school pitcher you can review and learn information that will help you take your game to a higher level. For young pitchers just learning the game, the information contained within each chapter will allow you to understand all the concepts necessary for executing the position. For adults attempting to teach their young pitchers, the information within provides the right way to develop a young pitcher and the right steps to improve their skill levels.

Coaches can use this information to reinforce their pitching concepts and to further develop their pitching knowledge. As a coach, I find that there is always more to learn about the art of pitching. The amount of knowledge and level of physical skill required of a pitcher makes it more difficult to teach pitching than any other baseball activity. It takes years of commitment on the part of the player to develop and become a successful high school pitcher. Young pitchers are easily discouraged by poor performances and drop out of baseball. Pitching is not for everyone! Even mastering all the information contained in this document will not guarantee success. However, it will assist in achieving a high level of pitching knowledge regardless of the physical abilities of the individual.

It is difficult to find in one place all the information contained in this book. There are an infinite number of resources available about the art of pitching. These include books, presentations, videos, the Internet, and other resources. The information presented in this book is provided for youth at all levels of play. Some information is basic, other descriptions are quite detailed giving the reader a vast range for understanding the concepts involved with pitching. All chapters attempt to provide the basic concepts and then go further with detailed information about the principles behind each concept. Additionally, there is a large emphasis on correcting and adjusting common issues and the best approach to improving performance.

It will be difficult for all the information to be absorbed in a single reading. Each section has been written such that reference to a given topic can be read or reviewed without requiring reading the entire book. In other words, the book can be used as a reference for specific topics (by chapter) and referred to when working on a specific aspect of the game. For most, it is recommended to read the entire book and then use the desired concept material as a reference. Ideally it would be desirable to have graphic images to support the text and provide descriptive visual information. Included are several pictures, charts and drawings that attempt to visualize some of the information presented in the text. In many cases, additional drawings would be helpful and are planned for future editions.

Chapter II:

Pitching General Philosophy

Good pitchers follow general pitching guidelines to be effective. Obviously, the quality of the pitcher and batter, as well as the game situation dictate how to approach pitching to a specific hitter. However, in general there are several key pitching philosophies that have been proven to be successful. Remember that these are general concepts and, as there are many variables in a game, situations may require deviation from these goals. The following discussion presents the concepts and examines the relevant reasoning behind each concept.

1) FIRST PITCH STRIKES: The target for most pitches thrown should be a strike. This can be deviated from when the count is heavily in favor of the pitcher, but throwing strikes is important at all levels of play. To that end, the first pitch thrown to a batter should always be a strike. Not only does this immediately place the pitcher at an advantage, but statistics have shown that batting averages go down when the pitcher is ahead in the count. Getting ahead in the count early also reduces the likelihood of a walk and, on average, reduces the chances of good contact by the batter. Many batters will always take the first pitch. Your pitch count will be reduced if you throw first pitch strikes. Throw your most accurate pitch (probably a fastball) until the batters start swinging on the first pitch; then mix in your best off-speed pitch as your first pitch but still throw strikes!

2) HAVE A TARGET: Have a target in your mind as part of the pitch type. This means a pitch type and a pitch location should be embedded in your head before you throw your pitch. You always want to associate each pitch thrown with a location, speed, and movement. Note that location is listed first as it is the most important characteristic of any pitch. To help with location, the catcher should set their glove at the desired location as the pitcher's target. To simplify pitch location and communication with the catcher, a signal system can be used. For example, a good way to think of a pitch location is to use a Horizontal Pitch Scheme as described below:

Four Zone Horizontal Pitch Scheme
From left to right, (as the catcher sees the pitch) there are 4 horizontal pitching target zones.

1. ZONE #1 - Eight (8) inches left of the plate to the left edge of home plate.
2. ZONE #2 – Left edge of the plate to the middle of home plate.
3. ZONE #3 – Middle of plate to the right edge of home plate.
4. ZONE #4 – Right edge of plate to eight (8) inches right of home plate.

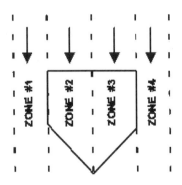

Most pitches should be directed toward ZONES 2 and 3. Zones 1 and 4 are used when ahead in the count or pitching around a batter. The vertical location for pitches should be one of two places, at the knees or at the letters. Using the zone concept can be helpful in calling pitches and relaying information between coaches, catchers, and pitchers.

3) PITCH AT THE KNEES/LETTERS: Most hitters make less contact with the baseball with pitches thrown at the low or high vertical ends of the strike zone. Keeping the ball down minimizes line drives and deep fly balls. It also induces ground balls which are ideal when a double play is needed. Generally, ground balls are either outs or at most singles. Most batters have a hard time hitting low pitches with power. Umpires have a hard time calling border line low pitches anything but strikes unless they are in the dirt. Additionally, working up and down usually sets up a high pitch for either a routine fly ball or a swing and miss. Pitches at the letters usually induce fly balls or swings and misses.

4) CHALLENGE HITTERS – LET YOUR FIELDERS PLAY DEFENSE: We do not need or want to strike everyone out. Trying to strike out batters requires a lot of pitches leading to fatigue and takes the pitcher out of the game in the later innings. Your goal should be to 'Pitch to Contact' and MINIMIZE YOUR WALKS! Let your fielders make plays as it keeps their heads in the game and YOU!

5) YOUR GOAL-NO WALKS! - Our goal is NO FREE PASSES! This is probably not realistic, but we need to minimize walks per game. If you walk two or less batters per game, odds are you will win! Walks can be minimized by getting ahead in the count – challenge hitters! Throw strikes!

6) FOLLOW THE 'LMV' CONCEPT – What constitutes an effective pitch? What thrown baseball actions are most important for the success of a pitch? Simply put, what are the characteristics that make a pitch difficult to hit? They are, in order of importance, Location(L), Movement(M) and Velocity(V). These three characteristics constitute the LMV Concept for any thrown pitch. That is, the effectiveness of any pitch is a function of its location, movement, and velocity. Note that location is listed first, movement second and velocity last!

7) BE MENTALLY TOUGH – All pitchers give up hits, they walk batters, they hit batters, they give up extra base hits and homeruns. This is part of the game and should not be considered a sign of failure. Batters strike out, hit into double plays, and lay down terrible bunts. But when they come up to bat the next time, they put their previous at bat behind them because it is a whole new situation. Again, this is part of the game and to be successful the last bad pitch thrown must be forgotten and the focus placed on the next pitch. A pitcher that shows frustration on the mound is mentally and physically affected. How many times has a pitcher been mowing down batters, maybe even a perfect game, and a hit or fielding error occurs? The next thing you know the pitcher is falling behind in the count, giving up hits, walking batters and struggling to get back in the groove. This clearly is a mental let-down on the part of the pitcher. It is important to stay focused, understand that each pitch is important and that your team and the opponent can see your frustration.

8) ADAPT TO THE UMPIRE – Each umpire has a slightly different strike zone. Be prepared to adjust your targets to benefit from the strike zone for that game. If slightly outside pitches are called strikes, use that to your advantage. Typically, the normal edges of the strike zone will vary on any given day. Work the edges that seem

expanded and stay away from those that seem squeezed even if that was your original game plan.

9) BE A FIELDER – Your role as a pitcher changes once the ball is put in play. Field your position, backup bases and show both teams that you know your responsibilities after the pitch has been thrown. You will be surprised how that slows down your opponent's base running game.

10) MAKE ADJUSTMENTS WHILE ON THE MOUND – Understanding the potential flaws in your throwing motion is important such that you can adjust your mechanics if necessary. Most mounds are slightly different even though there are specific guidelines to their layout. High or low mounds may require a pitcher to adjust their mechanics to accommodate the height deviation. Holes in the landing area or in front of the rubber often cause havoc with the stride. Even the physical condition of the pitcher, feeling tired or strong, may require adjustment to a pitcher's throwing motion. If you are consistently missing high, or low, or outside, etc., you should be able to recognize the issue and make corrections.

By following these simple concepts, a pitcher can be successful at any level. Learning to deal with adversity and making adjustments is a requirement for any successful pitcher. Just by taking the actions that a skilled and knowledgeable pitcher would take gives you a distinct advantage on the field.

A story was once told about a famous pitcher by the name of Nolan Ryan. The tale typifies overcoming pitching adversity and having mental toughness. Known as a fast ball pitcher (the Ryan Express) with amazing skills, Nolan Ryan was a dominating Major League pitcher for many years. He pitched seven no-hit games and twelve one-hit games in twenty-seven Major League seasons. So, here is the story:

While warming-up in the bullpen prior to the start of a game, Nolan Ryan turned to his pitching coach and said, "It's going to be a tough day, I ain't got anything." He then proceeded to go out that day and pitch a no hitter!

Chapter III:

Pitching Mechanics

When throwing a pitch, the actions of a pitcher are known as the pitcher's mechanics. Ideally, the mechanics of a pitcher are close to identical from pitch to pitch. Every pitcher throws with slightly different mechanics. However, there are specifics to the throwing motion that have been shown to produce optimal results. A pitcher's mechanics dictate not only the velocity of a thrown pitch, but also its accuracy (or location). Thus, a pitcher with 'good' mechanics has a repeatable series of motions that fall close to known optimal throwing actions.

Although pitchers have different motions, the ultimate determination as to what part of their mechanics should be corrected is directly related to their throwing accuracy, their velocity, and their ability to limit physical injury. Most young, developing pitchers today have problems with accuracy (throwing strikes consistently) and therefore every attempt should be made to develop proper mechanics. Most high school pitchers are inconsistent at best, and their motion tends to limit pitch types as well as velocity and accuracy.

The following provides descriptive information that is widely accepted as the 'correct' pitching mechanics. There are a few areas where some differences of opinion may exist about the presented pitching actions. However, for the most part, the pitching motions presented below are mainstream and widely accepted as the most effective pitching mechanics.

There are two primary modes of pitching: (1) Pitching from the Windup and (2) Pitching from the Stretch. Pitchers throw from the windup when there are no runners on base. The Stretch mode is used whenever there are one or more runners on base. For most pitchers, the windup motion typically provides a slight increase in velocity and accuracy. However, since the motion of the windup takes time, it offers baserunners an advantage for stealing a base. Therefore, pitching from the windup is not typically used with runners on base. Pitching from the stretch is a faster motion that allows runners to be held more effectively, but typically with slightly decreased pitch speed and accuracy. Pickoff throws to bases to discourage runners from stealing can only be made when the pitcher is throwing from the stretch position. The proper pitching mechanics for delivering a pitch from the windup and stretch positions are described below:

A. Pitching from the Windup

1) Starting Position
    a) Feet – Shoulder width, arch of feet or heels on the front edge of the rubber.
    b) Hands – Baseball in glove, glove just below chin. Throwing hand loosely holding the ball.
    c) Shoulders – Square with catcher.
    d) Eyes – Focused on target (catcher's glove or signaling hand).
    e) The pitcher should now take signs from the catcher.
2) Weight Shift – (Moving Pivot foot to the front edge of the rubber)
    a) Left Foot* - Takes a small step (4"- 8") to the left just off the side of the pitching rubber. The weight is now shifted to this foot upon landing.

b) Right Foot* – (Pivot foot) - Lift slightly and rotate 90°. Then place the foot directly in front of the pitching rubber with the side edge of the foot now in contact with the front edge of the pitching rubber. *NOTE: There must be contact between the pivot foot and the plate for all thrown pitches.*

*For RH pitcher; opposite if LH pitchers
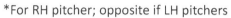

3) Leg Lift – Leg Drop

a) The non-pivot foot leg (stride leg) is lifted straight up to 90° (parallel to ground and pivot foot) and then lowered straight down to within 1 or 2 inches of the mound surface.

b) The stride foot should be hanging loose and <u>not</u> held in a ridged position as the foot moves up and then down.

c) The hands and arms remain in their position as the leg lift occurs.

d) As the stride leg drops down, both elbows start their swing back/forward away from the body and the forearms and hands swing back/forward from the elbows. Both elbows swing to shoulder height. The forearms and hands also swing close to shoulder height. This process ends when the stride foot lands.

e) When the baseball is extended fully to the back, the fingers on the ball hand should point down (palm down) and be located directly behind the pitcher, but not angled behind the pitcher's back.

f) The front arm and glove hand point straight toward the catcher (target).

g) At this time, for alignment purposes, you should think of a straight line that could be drawn from the catcher's glove through the pitcher's glove and shoulders and back to the pitcher's throwing hand.

4) Stride

a) After the stride foot drops straight down to within 1"-2" of the mound surface, the stride leg and foot drives (accelerates) out, directly toward home plate and just inches above the mound surface. (This action is called 'Drop and Drive'.)

b) The pivot leg, with minimal knee bend, is used to drive (accelerate) the stride leg forward.

c) Just prior to the stride foot landing, the back hip begins its forward rotation (acceleration).

d) Upon landing, the stride foot should point toward home plate or be slightly closed (less than 15 degrees).

e) The stride foot should land on a line toward the target.

f) After the stride step landing, the back shoulder immediately starts to rotate initiated by the hip rotation, eventually placing both shoulders in a perpendicular relationship to home plate (shoulders should not over- or under-rotate). This rotation is aided by the hip rotation (which started earlier) and creates torque through the pitcher's torso.

g) As the back shoulder begins to rotate, the pitching arm starts forward with the elbow leading.

5) Pitch

a) The arm starts forward with the elbow driving ahead. The ball hand stays back during the initial forward motion loading the forearm and ball hand. The hand rotates from palm down to palm up.

b) The shoulders should remain level during pitch delivery. However, the back shoulder does drive forward as the elbow drives forward.

c) As the pitching arm drives forward, the back is arched, and the front glove hand is pulled back slightly to meet the chest as it drives forward.

d) The pitching arm continues to drive forward with acceleration as the lower arm snaps forward followed by a wrist snap and arm finish down toward the front knee.

e) The preferred arm slot is 'Over the Top' or three-quarter motion with the ball passing somewhat close to the ear. This arm slot greatly assists the spin production of breaking balls.

f) The upper body bends at the waist and extends forward out over the front leg.

g) Both feet remain in contact with the mound until just before the ball is released.

h) The ball is released as far in front of body as possible without the hand dropping below the height of the pitching arm shoulder. This is the release point of the pitch.

i) For best results, focus on a consistent arm motion as close to ¾ over the top as possible – no sidearm throws!

NOTE: The ball is always taken back to the same position and the arm slot (arm motion forward) should always be the same!

6) Follow-through

a) The back leg (pivot leg) should not drag, but swing up and around, landing directly across from the stride foot.

b) Falling left or right after the pitch is thrown indicates that the stride was not far enough out (fall to the left) or too far out (fall to the right) *

   * Opposite for LH pitchers

c) The glove hand should finish in front of or next to the chest – not hanging down or out to the side. In the correct position, the glove will be in front of the 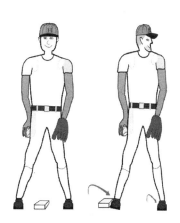 body in a position to field a hit ball. Your throwing hand should finish down and near your stride foot knee. Finishing at the waist or higher is an indication of a side arm throw and this action will cause the thrown baseball to miss right or left depending on the release point of the pitch.

B. **Pitching from the Stretch** – *Instruction for RH pitcher; opposite for LH pitcher*

1) Starting Position

   a) With the baseball in your throwing hand, straddle the rubber placing your left foot in front of rubber (1 - 2 feet), and your right foot behind the rubber but not in contact with the rubber. *(Classifies the player as a fielder.)*

b) Check any on-base runners, the position and readiness of fielders, the catcher, umpire, and coaches.

c) Lift your back foot (pivot foot) and place it in front of the pitching rubber such that the outside edge of the pivot foot is in contact with the front edge of the rubber. *(Classifies the player now as a pitcher.)*

d) The shoulders should be in line with the catcher, pointing along a target line to home plate.

e) Hold the ball in the throwing hand and let the throwing arm extend down from the back shoulder with the hand behind the back leg.

f) The glove arm can hang loosely, straight down from the front shoulder or rest on the front knee.

g) The pitcher then takes the pitch (or special defensive play) signs from the catcher.

h) The pitcher should check any runners. During this phase, the head and shoulders can move.

2) Set Position

a) Both hands are brought up together to a point just below the chin with the ball in the throwing hand and hidden loosely in the glove. (This is the SET POSITION).

b) At the same time, the stride leg/foot is brought straight back to within 6" to 8" of the pivot foot.

c) The pitch grip is now adjusted to throw the desired pitch using minimal motion.

d) Base runners are checked (only the head can move).

e) Just before the forward pitching motion starts, a 'NOTICEABLE PAUSE' must occur.

f) The pitcher should vary the 'PAUSE' time of each pitch to freeze runners.

g) If a runner breaks, the pitcher's first move must be to step back off the rubber with the pivot foot. Then he can act like a fielder.

h) The pitcher may step back off the rubber with their pivot foot at any time to become a fielder.

3) Drive and Load

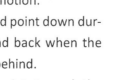

a) Your weight shifts to the back leg (pivot).

b) The front leg (stride) <u>drives</u> forward as a 'slide step'. (NO LEG LIFT)

c) During the slide step, both elbows are driven away from the body and the hands swing outward, elbows to shoulder height. This is a rapid but smooth motion.

d) Fingers on the ball hand point down during the arm swing, and back when the arm is fully extended behind.

e) The front hand (glove) points towards the catcher (target).

4) Pitch (same as windup)

a) The arm drives forward with the elbow leading. The ball hand stays back during the initial forward motion loading the forearm and ball hand.

b) The shoulders should remain level during pitch delivery. However, the back shoulder does drive forward as the elbow drives forward.

c) As the pitching arm drives forward, the back is arched, and the front glove hand is pulled back slightly to meet the chest as it drives forward.

d) The pitching arm continues to drive forward with acceleration as the upper arm snaps forward followed by a wrist snap and the arm finishing down towards the front knee.

e) The preferred arm slot is 'Over the Top' or ¾ motion with the ball passing somewhat close to the ear.

f) Both feet remain in contact with the mound until the ball is released.

g) The upper body bends at the waist and extends out over the front leg.

h) The ball is released as far in front of body as possible without dropping below the height 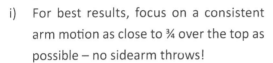 of the pitching arm shoulder. This is the release point of the pitch.

i) For best results, focus on a consistent arm motion as close to ¾ over the top as possible – no sidearm throws!

5) Follow-through (same as windup motion).

a) The back leg (pivot leg) should not drag, but swing up and around, landing directly across from the stride foot.

b) Falling left or right after the pitch is thrown indicates that the stride was not far enough out (fall to the left) or too far out (fall to the right) *

   * Opposite for LH pitchers

c) The glove hand should finish in front of or next to the chest but not hanging down or out to the side. In the correct position, the glove will be in front of the body in a position  to field a hit ball.

Chapter IV:

Identifying and Correcting Mechanical Flaws

Now that a discussion regarding best pitching mechanics has been presented, it would be advantageous to examine common flaws and their solutions. Every pitcher should work to adjust their mechanics based on their individual velocity and accuracy deficiencies. Mechanical flaws can then be identified and corrected. It is difficult for most pitchers to self-assess their throwing mechanics and this is where a knowledgeable coach can be of great assistance. Video recording is an excellent method of assessing a pitcher's mechanics. The use of slow-motion video from different directions to demonstrate to the pitcher throwing issues allows for self-assessment by the pitcher. Comparisons can be made between a pitcher's mechanics and the mechanics of a pitcher with good throwing mechanics. Pitchers with poor mechanics usually have inconsistent pitching performances.

Analysis of the path of a thrown ball as well as its velocity and final pitch location will help identify some of a pitcher's mechanical issues. However, direct viewing of a pitcher's motion usually is sufficient to identify why a pitcher is struggling with a specific issue. Pitching problems typically deal with accuracy, inconsistency, the lack of velocity, the lack of spin or just the inability to throw strikes! The following information is a discussion of typical pitching issues that can be directly tied back to a mechanical flaw. Many of these can be easily identified and corrected by adjusting to the best practice pitching mechanics.

Understanding Your Mechanics

1) Missing the Strike Zone Up or Down
   a) Missing Up – A vertical adjustment to pitch location can be made by:
      i. Lowering the front side: By lowering the glove arm when extended forward, the pitch will be lower. This requires only a subtle adjustment to the glove arm. Lower it when extended about 1 to 3 inches. This action works because lowering the glove arm means that the throwing arm will be higher behind you resulting in a pitch that is thrown lower.
      ii. Leveling the shoulders so that they point directly at the target. A high front shoulder causes a high pitch. Point your extended glove arm at your target. This will typically lower your front side.
      iii. Releasing the ball too early will cause the pitch to miss high – all pitches must be released as far in front as possible. Find your release point. It is typically at the extended throwing arm point where the hand starts to drop below your shoulder height.
   b) Missing Down – A vertical adjustment to pitch location can be made by:
      i. Standing tall - Bending the knees during the wind-up motion lowers your entire body and typically causes the ball to be short of the target. Stand tall and throw downhill, down the mound to maximize pitch speed. Lowering your body takes away the downhill advantage!
      ii. Leveling the shoulders so that they point directly at the target. A low front shoulder may cause a pitch to be low. Point your extended glove arm at your target. This will typically raise your front side.
      iii. Raising the front side: That is by raising the glove arm when extended forward, the pitch will be higher. This requires only a subtle adjustment to the glove arm. Raise it when extended about 1 to 3 inches. This action works because raising the

glove arm means that the throwing arm will be lower behind you resulting in a pitch that is thrown higher.

2) Missing the Strike Zone Left or Right

   a) A side-arm motion typically results in missing the target left or right since you are throwing across your body. The throwing arm slot should be closer to a ¾ motion. If you finish 'OUT and DOWN', you will not throw with a 'side to side' movement in your arm motion, thus reducing the likelihood of missing your target left or right.

   b) Side-arm throwers add a side-to-side component to forward velocity. That causes the baseball to move right or left depending on the point of release.

   c) Side-arm throwers often release the baseball with a wrist motion that causes spin rotation and the thrown baseball to break right or left. This makes accuracy difficult. Side arm pitchers often hit batters because of the difficulty in controlling the spin.

   d) Shoulder rotation more than square or 90 degrees prior to releases will cause the ball to be thrown left or right of the target. *(NOTE: Shoulder extension may look like over rotation, but it is beneficial and should not be corrected.)*

   e) A stride foot landing to the side of an imaginary line drawn from the pitching rubber to the catcher will cause pitches to land right and left of their expected target. This offset landing is also an indicator of poor hip rotation or over rotation.

   f) A stride foot upon landing that is too open or closed can cause misses left and right.

   g) An unbalanced or short stride foot landing causing falling to the left or right contributes to misses to the sides of the plate.

   h) Taking the ball back behind you rather than straight back will cause side to side variations in the pitch location. This take back problem also results in shoulder rotation when the pitch is made.

3) Missing with Your Specialty Pitches

   a) When throwing the curve ball, it is not uncommon to pull the arm down when attempting to put over-the-top spin on the pitch. The key to resolving this problem is to realize that only the wrist snaps down, not the throwing arm. The arm slot must remain the same for all pitches, even off-speed pitches.

b) When throwing changeups, the grip is such that the release can be difficult. The tendency is to hold the ball past the normal release point such that the ball comes out of the hand late and when the arm is lowering. This results in a pitch that bounces into the catcher. Work on releasing the ball at your normal release point.

c) Sliders move right to left and down for right hand pitchers. Many outside corner sliders 'hang' and do not break, ending up over the center of the plate, and often hitting batters. Work on a consistent release of this pitch such that the spin is close to the same with every thrown slider.

d) The high fastball can be a very effective pitch. However, many young pitchers fail to practice their high fastball, and this results in either wasted pitches or pitches down the center of the plate. Learn how to consistently throw a high fastball. You can do this by shortening your stride step or raising your front glove slightly. Either or both of these two actions should result in a high pitch – practice to achieve control of the accuracy! High fastballs help disguise your curve ball.

e) Tailing fastball pitches are a direct result of your grip. These pitches can be a great weapon if you understand how and why your pitch tails. For right handers, a tailing pitch breaks right, into a right-hand batter. Left hand pitchers have a tail that breaks away from the right-hand batter. So, what causes a fastball to tail? Primarily, it is your grip at release. When your top two fingers move off the top and at release are on the side of the baseball, your wrist snap puts side spin on the baseball which causes a tailing movement. To reduce or eliminate tailing, keep your wrist in a position such that your top two fingers at release are directly on top of the ball.

Making changes to your pitching mechanics can alleviate many throwing issues. Pitch movement, location and velocity can be improved. Always start with the basics and work your way into more detailed and difficult corrections. Make sure that you can throw your fastball with accuracy and speed before assuming that your mechanics are solid and throwing other pitch types will be successful. Every pitching experience will be different. Learn to make adjustments on the mound using your knowledge of the problem on that given day. Once a deficiency has been identified, use drills and repetitions to adapt to the proper mechanics.

Answering Questions About Proper Pitching Mechanics:

1. **Where should my feet be located on the pitching rubber when I throw from the windup?**
   Your feet should be shoulder width apart with both heels on the pitching rubber, toes forward. You can move the starting position of your feet left or right on the rubber, whatever feels most comfortable for your throwing angle to the plate.

2. **Where should my feet be located on the pitching rubber when I throw from the stretch?**
   When starting your motion from the stretch, only your pivot foot is in contact with the pitching rubber. Select a comfortable contact position on the rubber. Your stride foot should be 12 to 16 inches in front of the rubber on an imaginary line toward home plate. With a runner on first, open your stride foot location to assist in throwing over to first to hold the runner.

3. **When I start my motion, where should my glove be? How about my throwing hand?**
   In both the windup and stretch starting positions, your glove should be just below your chin and your throwing hand should be holding the baseball in your glove.

4. **When throwing from the windup, where do I step to start my pitching motion?**

    With your stride foot, step about 2 to 6 inches directly to your left. The step is small to minimize head and torso movement. Keep your eyes focused on your target. Remember, the only reason for this step is to transfer your weight and allow your pivot foot to be moved to the front edge of the pitching rubber.

5. **Where should my pivot foot be with respect to the pitching rubber?**

    The outside edge of your pivot foot always gets placed against the front edge of the pitching rubber. NOT ON the rubber! It can be anywhere along a line across the front edge of the rubber as long as some portion of your pivot foot is in contact with the rubber. Your entire pivot foot edge does not have to be in contact, just some portion of your pivot foot.

6. **How high should I lift my stride leg when throwing from the windup?**

    Your stride leg lifts straight up (foot dangling) until your thigh is at 90 degrees to your body. You lift to this point since it is easy to duplicate; each leg lift should be to a consistent location to standardize the timing of your movements during your throwing motion.

7. **Should I lift my stride leg when throwing from the stretch?**

    NO! Most likely there are runners on base and lifting your stride leg as you do from the windup would give the runners extra time to steal a base or take a large lead. Use a slide step motion to speed up your delivery to the plate.

8. **How should I take my throwing arm back?**

    Take your throwing arm straight back as far as you can with your palm pointing down. Think about trying to touch a wall behind you and extending your arm. Do not short arm your throw. Do not let your shoulders rotate. Both shoulders should be aligned and directed along an imaginary line toward home plate. Any shoulder rotation will cause the ball to be taken back behind your body. This causes rotation in your shoulders as you try to align your shoulders during the forward throwing motion.

9. **Why do you drive your elbow when starting your forward throwing motion?**

When you drive your arm forward to throw, you must accelerate the throwing arm to develop pitch speed. Driving the elbow first allows the forearm to be accelerated (whipped) about the elbow. Most pitchers who throw with high velocities drive their elbows such that their forearm lags behind parallel to the ground.

10. **How should my stride foot land?**

Your stride foot should land softly along an imaginary line from your pivot foot to the catcher. It should land either pointing directly at the catcher or slightly closed. If it lands open, then your hips have over-rotated, and you will have side to side movement in your mechanics.

11. **How far should I stride out?**

Stride out as far as you can. If you fall to your glove side after releasing the baseball, your stride is probably too short. Ideally, your trailing leg/foot lands at about the same distance in front of the rubber as your stride foot. It is acceptable if your stride foot is slightly ahead of your trailing foot, but not the other way around.

12. **How do I drop my leg after lifting it to 90 degrees?**

The drop motion is smooth and steady. The leg/foot drops straight down to within 2 to3 inches of the mound. Do not let the leg fall forward. This is a gravity fall forward and it reduces your ability to drive or explode pushing off the rubber with your pivot leg/foot.

Drop straight down and then explode forward driving your hips and leg/foot down the mound.

13. How do I drive my stride foot down the mound?

After dropping straight down within 2 to 3 inches of the mound, push with your pivot leg and explode forward driving your leg/foot down the mound (just above the mound by 2 to3 inches) and land softly.

14. How should I finish my throwing motion?

Finish your throwing motion thinking 'out and down'. Bend at the waist and extend out over your stride leg. After releasing the base-ball with your throwing arm, finish downward toward your stride leg knee. Your glove should stay in front of your chest. Do not let your glove drop or fall behind your body. This causes shoulder rotation and leaves the pitcher in a poor fielding position, especially for line drives!

Chapter V:

Pitch Types

As described earlier, the effectiveness of a pitch is a function of location, movement, and velocity. Movement can be achieved by using the physical properties of a baseball to create changes in the perceived path of a thrown baseball. By design, a baseball has seams that protrude slightly from the surface of the ball. When thrown, the baseball's direction is affected by the seams. Since the seams ride above the relatively smooth surface of a baseball, the seams cause friction or drag with respect to the air passing by. This drag results in movement of the baseball as it travels through the air. By spinning the baseball in a specific pattern, control of the resulting ball movement can be achieved. Thus, different baseball movements or pitch types have been developed to create pitches that break and are more difficult to hit.

When throwing a pitch, the off-line movement of a baseball is a function of the spin and seam locations of the ball as it travels through the air to home plate. Movement of the baseball either to the left, right or down is a function of the direction of spin. A forward or over the top spin causes the baseball to break downward. Side spin causes the ball to move left or right. The spin rate is developed by the snap of the wrist. The faster the spin rate, the more break or movement of the baseball. The spin axis controls the direction of break. The wrist position at release dictates the direction of spin (alignment of the spin axis).

The spin of a baseball causes changes in the final direction of a thrown baseball primarily due to the air friction or 'drag' that occurs on the side of the ball where the spin opposes the direction of the throw. Figure V-1 demonstrates this phenomenon for a four-seam fastball. Note that the seams on the bottom of the baseball are spinning in opposition to the air as the baseball moves toward home plate. This drag (air resistance) slightly slows the air movement below the baseball. A slower air movement causes a higher air pressure to develop under the ball. On the top of the ball, the seams are moving in a direction that assists the air displacement which creates less of a drag and therefore a lower air pressure on top of the ball. The baseball wants to move up toward the area with a lower pressure. This allows the ball to fight the effects of gravity and appear to rise or stay at the same height throughout the throw. Thus, it is shown that by spinning the baseball seams in a specific direction, we can create a pressure differential that causes the baseball to curve or appear to move in a specific direction.

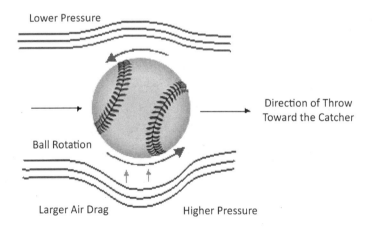

Figure V-1: Four Seam Fastball Spin and Movement

Pitch Types: Focus on 5 pitch types, proficiency priority from A to E:

A. <u>**Four Seam Fastball:**</u>

    1. For a proper grip, the ball is held in your fingers as shown in Figure V-2.

2. Fingers are across the seams so as the baseball spins it shows four seams.
3. There should be a visible gap between the baseball and inside hand web.
4. Spin at release is created by a wrist snap.
5. The spin direction is controlled by your wrist angle at release.
6. The baseball releases off the fingertips causing backspin on the thrown baseball.

Figure V-2: Four Seam Fastball Grip

B. Two Seam Fastball
1. For a proper grip, the ball is held in your fingers as shown in Figure V-3.
2. Fingers are on the seams so as the baseball spins it shows two seams.
3. There should be a visible gap between the baseball and inside hand.
4. Spin at release is created by a wrist snap.
5. The spin direction is controlled by your wrist angle at release.
6. The baseball releases off the fingertips causing backspin on the thrown baseball.
7. The grip creates a distinct movement from the four-seam fastball due to a different seam spin.

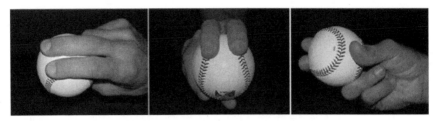

Figure V-3: Two Seam Fastball Grip

C. Change-Up

1. A Circle Change grip is preferred due to simplicity (See Figure V-4).
2. The ball is held by the outer 3 fingers and the thumb/index finger 'circle'.
3. The wrist is rotated slightly inward on ball release.
4. There should be minimal to no visible gap between the ball and hand.

Figure V-4: Change-up Grip

D. Curve

1. The ball is primarily held by the thumb and middle finger.
2. There is NO visible gap between the ball and hand web.
3. For the curve ball grip, the wrist is rotated to a 90-degree position prior to ball release. The ball points at the ear as it passes by (Figures V-5 and V-6).
4. The ball is released (snapped downward) off the side of the middle finger causing over-spin on the baseball.
5. The arm slot drives the hand close to the head with the elbow at shoulder height.

6. The ball at release is snapped downward using the wrist only and not the arm.

Figure V-5: Grip for a Beginner's Curveball

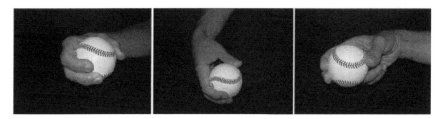

Figure V-6: Normal Curve Ball Grip

E. **Slider**

1. The grip requires the ball to be held in a similar fashion to a two-seam fastball.
2. The grip uses 2 fingers and the thumb, just like a two-seam fastball.
3. The difference is that the index finger is moved over next to the middle finger which is on the right (LHP-left) ball seam.
4. There should be a visible gap between the ball and hand web.
5. The wrist snap and wrist angle are the same as a two-seam fastball.
6. The baseball is released off the fingertips with a pull-down action of the fingers.
7. Since the fingers are on the side of the ball, a side spin is developed.

Figure V-7: Slider Grip

Each pitch type described should be thrown within a specified velocity range. The pitch speed attained is unique to each pitcher, however, their speed range for various pitch types should always be relative to the speed of their four-seam fastball. Below is Table V-1 which contains data for individual age groups, pitch types and their typically expected pitch speeds. Note that the speed of each pitch type is based on the speed of their four-seam fastball.

TABLE V-1:

Typical Pitch Speeds for Specific Pitch Types and the Pitcher's Age

Pitcher's Age Bracket	Four-Seam Fastball	Two-Seam Fastball	Changeup	Slider	Curve
10-12 Years	45-50 MPH	45-50 MPH	35-40 MPH	40-45 MPH	NA
13-14 Years	50-60 MPH	50-60 MPH	40-50 MPH	45-55 MPH	45-55 MPH
15-16 Years	60-75 MPH	60-75 MPH	50-65 MPH	55-70 MPH	55-70 MPH
17-18 Years	75-90 MPH	75-85 MPH	65-80 MPH	70-80 MPH	65-80 MPH

MPH = Miles Per Hour   NA=Not Appropriate

In general, pitch types follow the speed of the four-seam fastball. That is, all off-speed pitches should be less than the four-seam fastball and a percentage of their fastball. Changeups and curve balls should be 6-8 MPH slower than the four-seam fastball. Sliders should be 4-6 MPH below the speed of the fastball. Varying pitch speeds for a specific pitch type is not usually successful, but if the pitcher's mechanics can handle (with accuracy) a second speed variation, then two speeds of curve balls can be beneficial.

Using the three main components of a pitch: location, movement, and velocity (LMV), the pitcher can throw pitch types that are more difficult for the batter to make solid contact. All three components define every pitch and determine the overall effectiveness of the pitcher. Most pitchers will have varying control with different pitch types. The advantage of fast balls is that they typically have more accurate location as well as a high velocity. The disadvantage is that they are more of a straight pitch, so movement is minimized. Off speed pitches such as changeups, sliders, and curve balls have more movement, and this is where their advantage is observed. By mixing pitch types, the batter can be kept off balance. The pitcher must know which pitch type is best for the game situation and challenging the batter. This is also where a coach, calling pitches, can help the pitcher. Using changes in the LMV components will maximize the likelihood of a successful pitching performance.

Chapter VI:

Understanding Throwing Velocity

You often hear people talking about a **pitcher's velocity** – the desire to throw harder and faster. Professional pitchers who can throw above 95 mph are admired. High school pitchers that throw above 80 mph are considered exceptional. Coaches are always looking for the player with a 'gun for an arm'. However, the how and why some players throw harder than others are often misunderstood, and little is known on how to analyze a player's throwing motion to increase their throwing velocity safely and accurately. There is little discussion in the literature about how that velocity is actually developed. The following discussion will attempt to describe how the throwing motion of a baseball player determines the exit velocity of a thrown baseball.

There are many factors that contribute to the overall velocity of a thrown baseball. Primarily it is the movement of various muscle modules in a specific sequence that develops the overall velocity of a thrown baseball. We will identify and examine each one of these and attempt to rationalize the various contributions that each of these muscle groups make to the overall velocity of a thrown baseball. Because in baseball a pitcher throws with high velocity more times than any other player and with required accuracy, we will focus on a pitcher's motion, although such an analysis applies to any player who throws a baseball.

A baseball player's throwing motion can be described as a smooth sequence of muscle actions that are enacted so as to launch a hand-held baseball in a specific direction with a given amount of speed. These muscle actions accelerate the baseball and upon release determine the speed (velocity) of the thrown ball. Let us break down the throwing motion and identify the muscle groups that primarily contribute to the overall velocity of a thrown baseball. Figure VI-1 identifies six throwing actions and their sequence that are the primary contributors to a thrown baseball's exit velocity.

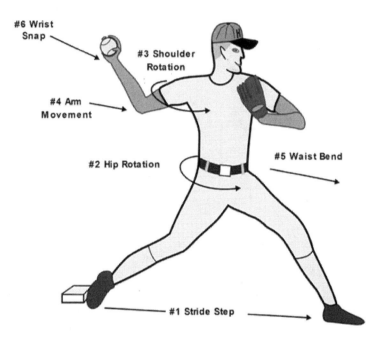

Figure VI-1: Muscle Sequences for a Thrown Baseball

The Muscle Groups: #1 Foot Stride

The throwing sequence begins at the feet with a stepping motion. This motion aligns the upper body such that the front shoulder of the non-throwing arm is in front, pointing directly at the target. The motion is a step forward toward the target initiating the body's first throwing movement. The step or stride provides the first energy component to developing the baseball's exit velocity upon release. It can be thought of as an acceleration process that begins the forward velocity development of the throwing motion. Take away the step (stride) and the throw will have a lower velocity. The contribution of the stride motion to the overall baseball exit velocity ranges from 0% to 15%. Smaller percentage contributions can be represented by throwing a baseball with NO STEP forward and then comparing it with the same body motion throwing with a step forward. The larger percentage contribution can also be exhibited by an outfielder throwing after catching a fly ball and taking a large "crow hop" in an effort to fire to a base or home plate. This forward motion accelerates the body and adds velocity to the throw. For a pitcher, we would expect to see a velocity contribution of 5% to 10% maximum.

NOTE: During the stepping motion (stride), the throwing arm is taken back to full extension with the ball in a grip of the throwing hand palm down. Although this is part of the throwing motion, it does not directly contribute to the exit velocity of a thrown baseball.

So, can a pitcher improve their throwing velocity by adjusting their stride? The answer is YES, but typically not significantly. If one compares a young pitcher to a high school pitcher, proper stride motion can make considerable improvements to velocity, but most experienced pitchers can only make small improvements to their overall velocity. Adjustments to a stride even for advanced pitchers can significantly help other performance factors such as accuracy and release speed and may also minimize physical stress and injury.

The Muscle Groups: #2 Hip Rotation

The next sequential movement in initiating a throw involves the hips. After striding forward toward the target, the hips must rotate 90 degrees for the upper body to square up with the target. This allows the upper body to directly face the target and permits the necessary arm motion required to launch the ball forward. The hip rotation only contributes 5% to 10% of the baseball's exit velocity. It does this indirectly as the hip rotation allows the shoulder of the throwing arm to rotate and accelerate toward the target. The timing of the hip rotation is important. Hip rotation begins late in the stride step forward, just prior to the landing of the stride foot. This allows for some torque to develop between the feet, legs and hips providing rotational acceleration of the hips. Slightly after the front foot lands, the hips should be fully rotated (90 degrees) and facing the target.

So, can a pitcher improve their throwing velocity by adjusting their hip rotation? The answer is YES, but typically not significantly. Normally we see more meaningful contributions to pitchers with a larger upper body mass who are flexible and strong enough to be able to rotate their hips with some explosion. The reality of improving throwing velocity by increasing hip acceleration is difficult because of the timing nature of the hip rotation and the arm's throwing motion.

The Muscle Groups: #3 Shoulder Rotation

The next sequential movement in initiating a throwing motion involves the shoulder and the throwing arm. The pitcher's upper torso and throwing shoulder should now begin to rotate just slightly after the lower body's hip rotation begins. The hip rotation creates torque in the pitcher's frame and allows the shoulder to accelerate during its rotation. This acceleration begins the direct development of the baseball's forward velocity. In reality, we could add the velocity of the forward stride, the velocity generated at the end of hip rotation and the velocity created by shoulder rotation and call that velocity our initial thrown ball velocity, V_{init}. Shoulder rotation contributes 10% to 20% of the overall throwing velocity.

So, can a pitcher improve their throwing velocity by adjusting their shoulder rotation? The answer is YES, and it can be significant. Driving the shoulder with more acceleration can improve velocity, but it is a difficult concept for most young pitchers to grasp. A simpler concept may be to try to accelerate the whole arm movement sequence thus improving the shoulder rotation. Getting the timing down to a perfectly smooth and coordinated series of movements can improve the initial thrown ball velocity (V_{init}). Pitchers that improve the timing sequence of their hip motion and the intensity of their shoulder rotation can see significant improvement in their pitch velocity.

The Muscle Groups: #4 Arm Movement

Arm movement is the next sequential action of the overall throwing motion and is the major contributor for developing the velocity of a thrown baseball. Arm movement makes up 60% to 80% of a thrown ball's velocity. As the throwing arm accelerates forward, the elbow initially drives ahead of the ball hand such that the lower arm starts to approach a parallel relationship to the ground. This lagging hand motion creates potential energy in the throwing arm as the lower arm is now loaded much like a catapult ready for launch. It is the whipping action of the lower arm about the elbow joint and the driving motion of the upper arm about the shoulder that accelerates the ball. Driving the elbow forward and keeping the forearm back as much as possible can definitely increase the potential energy available during the arm snap process. The arm should continue to accelerate forward with extension to add velocity to the throw.

The velocity attributed to arm movement will be referred to as V_{arm} and it will always be a major contributor to the baseball's exit velocity, (V_{bb}). Ideally during arm movement, the baseball will continue to pick up velocity until its release.

So, can a pitcher improve their throwing velocity by accelerating their arm movement? Obviously YES. However, the ability to improve arm acceleration is very much constrained by the physical limitations of each individual player. Arm strengthening exercises combined with explosive movement work can improve V_{arm} as well as long toss and other throwing exercises. Experience shows that improvements more likely will come with age and maturity, but dedicated arm strengthening workouts clearly provide improved throwing velocity.

NOTE: It should be noted that proper throwing mechanics will always improve arm movement contributions to the exit velocity.

The Muscle Groups: #5 Torso Bend at Waist

During the end of the arm movement action, the waist is bent forward allowing the torso and arm to extend toward the plate. This action extends the time the arm can accelerate forward thus adding a small portion of velocity to the pitch. This added velocity is relatively small (3% to 5%) since the arm at extension is approaching a deceleration stage. At full extension, the arm starts to decelerate which aides in the release of the ball and the production of spin.

So, can a pitcher improve their throwing velocity by adjusting their torso bending at the waist? Probably not. However, by bending at the waist the pitch velocity is not negatively affected and the follow through can be completed with minimal strain on the arm. It is still recommended that the waist bend be significant to allow other accelerations not to be negatively affected. For the sake of clarity, we will call any velocity change due to bending of the waist V_{wb}. This velocity contribution will always be very close to zero and, for pitchers with poor mechanics could be negative. A negative velocity component ($-V_{wb}$) can be seen in pitchers that finish to the side rather than a waist bend forward.

The Muscle Groups: #6 Wrist Snap at Release

At the end of arm extension, the wrist is positioned and snapped to place a specific spin type on the released baseball. Any additional velocity, (which we label as V_{ws}), attributed to this snapping of the wrist is minimal (2% to 4%). However, the method of spin production, or lack of spin, does affect the speed of the thrown baseball. It is clear that different releases do affect the thrown baseball speed and it will always be a contributor to the baseball's exit velocity, (V_{bb}).

So, can a pitcher improve their throwing velocity by employing different spins on a released baseball? No, not really. More likely by placing various spins at release the exit velocity from the pitcher's hand will be reduced rather than increased. This results in a negative V_{ws} and is demonstrated by the release of curve balls and changeups that have reduced exit velocity. The only argument for some potential velocity increase, slight as it may be, is with the two and four seam fastballs as their releases involve a more natural movement of the wrist/hand.

Timing Sequence of the Six Muscle Groups

The beginning and end time points for each of the mentioned muscle groups is critical to the quality of the overall throwing motion and thus the exit velocity of a thrown baseball. Each muscle group must provide their contribution in a sequential format, some starting before others end and some lasting longer than others. The timing sequence of a typical thrown pitch from the windup is demonstrated in Figure VI-2. Note how each group relates to the others with regards to starting, stopping and duration. Although the overall timing will vary slightly with individual players, the relationship or sequence will be very similar.

Deviations from the typical sequence will affect the ability to maximize the baseball's exit velocity. Particular attention should be paid not only to the movements themselves, but to the start and finish of each. If identified, adjustments can be made in a player's timing sequence that will improve overall performance and exit velocity of a thrown baseball.

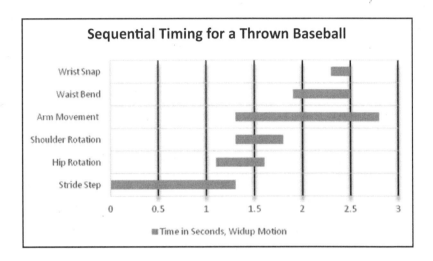

Figure VI-2: Sequential Timing for a Pitch from the Windup

NOTE: Times will be less for a pitch from the stretch, however the sequence remains the same.

Summarizing Muscle Sequences

The Velocity (Speed) of a thrown baseball is a function of several muscle groups with each one contributing some percentage of the baseball's exit velocity. As we have discussed, at release, the baseball's exit velocity (V_{bb}) is the sum of all forward contributing velocities:

$$V_{bb} = V_{init} + V_{arm} + V_{wb} + V_{ws}$$

where: V_{bb} = Speed of a Thrown Baseball

V_{int} = Initial Velocity Due to Muscle Groups #1, #2 and #3

V_{arm} = Velocity Component Due to Arm Throwing Motion

V_{wb} = Velocity Component Due to Waist Bend

V_{ws} = Velocity Component Due to Wrist Snap

Using average values from the ranges previously presented, we can represent the 6 contributions as:

Velocity of a Thrown Baseball V_{bb} 100% = (V_{init} 30%) + (V_{arm} 65%) + (V_{wb} 2%) + (V_{ws}3%)

The table below, Table VI-1, summarizes the various velocities we have discussed and their ranges of contribution to the overall speed of a thrown baseball. The typical percent contributions are common for high school pitchers.

Velocity Component Due to:	Label	% Range of Contribution to Exit Velocity	Sequential Phase	Typical % Contribution	Chance of Improving % Contribution
#1 Foot Stride	—	0% - 15%	1	8%	Fair
#2 Hip Rotation	—	5% - 10%	2	7%	Fair
#3 Shoulder Rotation	—	10% - 20%	3	15%	Minor
Muscle Groups #1 + #2 + #3	V_{int}	15% - 45%	1 - 3	30%	Fair
#4 Arm Throwing Motion	V_{arm}	60% - 80%	3	65%	Good
#5 Waist Bend	V_{wb}	3% - 5%	4	2%	Minor
#6 Wrist Snap	V_{ws}	2% - 4%	5	3%	Fair
ALL COMPONENTS (BB Velocity)	V_{bb}	NA	6	100%	NA

Table VI-1: Summary of Pitch Velocity Contributions and Improvement Probabilities

Other factors Affecting Throwing Velocity

There are many other factors that affect the velocity of a thrown base-ball. However, they are typically external conditions that are not specific to the player throwing the baseball. These include weather related conditions such as wind, rain, dampness, humidity, and air temperature. Field factors include such items as mound slope, mound height, ball weight (characteristics), ball seams and mound condition. Physical factors include pitch type, a tired arm, mental frustration, and other non-baseball related issues.

How to Improve Throwing Velocity – The Cruel Facts

Every baseball player wants to throw faster, more accurately and with consistency. Proper mechanics will always help with accuracy and consistency, and sometimes even velocity. However, for most pitchers, when it comes to throwing with increased velocity, the performance of one or more of the six muscle groups previously defined must be enhanced. By observing a player's throwing motion, it is easy to determine mechanical flaws that need to be corrected. However, it is much more difficult using observation to determine where performance can be improved to increase throwing velocity.

It is common to use video recordings of a throwing motion to review and correct mechanical flaws in the throwing motion. We speed up or slow down the video to view body and arm movements and show players what they need to do to improve their throwing mechanics. This process does not work well for determining the physical areas that could be enhanced to improve thrown baseball velocities. The cruel fact is that unless the observer has seen a lot of a pitcher's thrown baseballs, it is very difficult to advise where to focus improvement efforts.

The best plan for velocity improvement is to first focus on the player's basic throwing mechanics. Determine the adjustments needed and employ drills that correct the identified issues. It will take time and many repetitions to correct throwing flaws. Younger players tend to change their throwing motion as they physically grow. This gives great opportunity to make major throwing tweaks to their motion. Older, more experienced players have a harder time making major adjustments and a more focused single change seems to work more effectively. In any case, proper throwing mechanics should be the first priority to increasing throwing velocity.

Once the issues with mechanical flaws have been identified and addressed, an analysis of the six muscle groups that contribute to throwing velocity can be examined. Effort should be made to determine which muscle group performances need to be improved, with emphasis on the group that appears to be low in the % contribution range to overall velocity.

Specific Improvement Suggestions for Each Muscle Group

#1 Foot Stride – Stride velocity is a contributing factor to overall pitch speed. Accelerating the stride by driving off the rubber with the back pivot foot is key in developing positive impact on pitch velocity. Many pitchers simply fall forward when initiating their stride step. With this falling motion there is little acceleration developed resulting in a minimal contribution to the pitch velocity. Contrary to some beliefs, the length of stride is not a key factor for developing speed. Exploding or 'driving off' the back foot is what generates the energy to create forward velocity. Focus on the initial stride foot explosion to improve the foot stride velocity contribution.

#2 Hip Rotation – Hip rotation is the action that starts the generation of torso rotation. The timing of this movement is critical to the overall sequential timing of events during the throwing motion. Therefore, it is difficult to implement an increase in hip acceleration without affecting the timing of other time dependent actions during the throwing motion. Consequently, timing of the start of the hip rotation must be slightly adjusted (usually delayed) if acceleration is increased to improve the hip rotation velocity contribution.

#3 Shoulder Rotation – Shoulder rotation on the tossing arm side occurs as the throwing arm starts to move forward. The rotation that occurs is about an imaginary centerline drawn straight downward through the opposite shoulder. (*NOTE: This concept is contrary to popular belief that both shoulders rotate about a centerline drawn down through the center of the body, each shoulder moving in an opposite direction, one forward and one backward.*) The throwing arm shoulder literally accelerates the upper arm forward in a pulling motion until the arm is in line with both shoulders. During this process, the shoulder drive accelerates the throwing arm. With regards to overall timing, the hip movement first drives the torso and then the shoulder to rotate and this torquing action then initiates driving of the arm.

Accelerating the forward motion of the shoulder can assist in the development of additional arm speed. Again, think of initially driving the shoulder forward, pivoting about the opposite shoulder. This driving action improves the velocity of shoulder rotation.

#4 Arm Throwing Motion – The Arm Throwing Motion of a thrown baseball is a major contributor to the exit velocity of the baseball. It is therefore logical to think that this is the best place to improve the speed of a thrown baseball. Here are some improvement areas that can be examined:

1. Elbow Lead – Drive the elbow as early as possible during the throwing motion such that the forearm and hand lag behind. This allows for a 'whipping action' of the forearm once the elbow drive moves past the shoulder. Torso rotation completes with the upper body facing the target. The action of driving the elbow first as the

arm starts forward reinforces the benefits of the hand drag as described in 2 below.

2. Hand Drag - The hand drag creates stored or potential energy which can then be released to accelerate the forearm and generate velocity. This is an area to focus on if the hand with respect to the elbow does not achieve significant lag. Many hard throwing pitchers have a hand drag that causes their forearm (extending behind their elbow) to drop to a position that is actually parallel to the ground.

3. Whipping Action – Once the elbow lead has created a significant lag for the throwing hand, the forearm can be driven about the elbow creating a whipping action that accelerates the hand and forearm. The ability to accelerate this muscle activity varies with all players. However, with some strengthening work and focus on explosive forearm movement, the velocity generated can be improved.

4. Full Arm Extension – Full arm extension is necessary to direct all developed energy directly toward the target. Holding the ball and releasing it at the very end of full extension will achieve maximum velocity from the developed energy. The point of full extension is defined as the hand's forward location just before it begins to drop below the height of the shoulder. Think of a line (string) running from the throwing shoulder to the target. Full extension is when the hand just starts to drop below that line (string). *NOTE: This is also the **release point** of the throw.*

5. Finish Out and Down - Pulling the arm left or right during the finishing phase of throwing not only diminishes exit velocity but also accuracy. The correct finishing position for the throwing hand should be between the hip and knee. This can be achieved by throwing more 'over the top' or in other words, keeping the hand above the elbow and driving forward with the hand/elbow higher and the hand closer to the ear. Think finish out and down, not across the chest.

#5 Waist Bend – Bending of the waist is necessary to allow for all the developed velocity to be expended before deceleration factors slow the thrown baseball. The waist bend allows for full arm extension as well. Falling off to the side or throwing across the chest limits any waist drive contributions and even causes deceleration of the thrown ball. There are drills, such as touching the ground after throwing from the knees that help to reinforce waist bending. Also, long throws with crop hops from the outfield are good demonstrators of waist bending.

#6 Wrist Snap – Although we generally think of the wrist snap as contributing primarily to the spin of the baseball, there is clearly some velocity component as well. Two and four seam fastballs directly benefit from the wrist snap. Curveballs use the wrist snap more for rotational contributions rather than velocity. It is important that wrist snap occur at the end of full extension to maximize the contributions to spin and velocity. If video is available, slow the motion down and look for a wrist position that allows for some snapping action at the release point. Think, 'keep the wrist back' may help at times, but it is difficult for most young pitchers to execute.

Overall Summary – Understanding Throwing Velocity

The exit velocity of a thrown baseball is a function of six primary physical acceleration modules. The sequential action of these components each generate a contributing velocity that is added to generate the overall exit velocity of a thrown baseball. Realizing that only acceleration can increase velocity, it is the explosive action of each module that ultimately maximizes the velocity produced. During the pitching motion there are both acceleration and deceleration phases for each physical module. Sequencing these phases is important such that each deceleration phase does not affect the velocity of the pitch. Realizing that early action phases pass their generated velocities to later phases is important in understanding how velocity is generated during the pitching sequence. Attention must be made to the synchronization of each pitching module to maximize all velocity contributions.

Understanding how the exit velocity of a thrown baseball is developed should help in determining what actions are needed to improve the speed of a player's thrown baseball. Although the physical characteristics of each player clearly influences the maximum speed possible, by identifying the key muscle modules and their timing sequence, it is possible to make adjustments that can maximize any player's baseball throwing speed. Some suggestions have been made on how to approach the analysis and what areas can be focused on for improvement.

Chapter VII:

Pitching Smart

Pitch selection is important at higher levels of play. However, for younger pitchers, the fast ball is always the primary pitch (or only pitch) to throw. Most youth learn the fastball grips first and are discouraged by adults from throwing other pitch types for fear of physical damage to their arm, shoulder, or elbow. There are many opinions as to when it is a 'safe' age to throw off-speed pitches, that is pitches with spin. No matter where you fall with the argument, the reality is that young pitchers should focus on their mechanics rather than their pitch selection. Learning first how to throw a ball correctly will always minimize physical stress and injury. Focusing on proper mechanics will eventually result in pitchers throwing other pitch types with a greatly reduced potential for injury.

As pitchers develop it is normal for them to learn and understand that rotation, or spin, causes a thrown baseball to move or change its normal path. Eventually, they will be able to throw curve balls, changeups, sliders, and other off-speed pitches but it takes quite a while to master their accuracy. By the high school level, their precision normally improves such that these pitch types can be added to a pitcher's collection. However, this group of pitches is usually thrown with less accuracy and is not located consistently as desired. This leads to a lot of walks and hit batters which is common at the high school level. Knowing what pitch type to throw and when is an important component to the success of a pitcher. In a specific game situation, a pitcher must consider their pitching strengths as well as the game's situational factors when deciding on what pitch to throw.

Determining the best pitch to throw should include an analysis of the batter. Is the batter a power hitter or a line drive hitter? Does the batter show weakness opportunities in his stance or his swing? Does he pull the ball or is he late with his swings? Is he a fast runner, a threat to bunt? Is he a left-hand or right-hand batter? Is he tall or short? Where does he bat in the order? Does he swing at first pitches or mostly take one? Is he an aggressive hitter or does he seem to go deep in the count? Did he show any weakness with respect to pitch type in a previous at bat? Does it look like he is looking for a specific pitch or location? Does he ever swing at inside pitches or does he seem to back out? Can he be fooled by using a previous pitch to setup the next pitch? All these questions can help a pitcher determine what pitch to make and when to throw it. Unfortunately, it is difficult for most pitchers to assess batters while they are pitching. This is where a good catcher or coach can be of assistance as they have a better opportunity to evaluate the batter.

Determining the best pitch to throw should include the status of the inning. How many outs are there? Are there any base runners? What is the score? What inning is it? What is my goal for this hitter? Do I need a strikeout, a ground ball or any out? Can I challenge the batter without worrying about too much damage? Where are my strong fielders, left side, right side? Should I pitch around this batter? Should I load the bases hoping for a double play ball? Should I pitch down in the zone to try to get a ground ball? As a pitcher, you cannot rely on a strikeout to get you out of a jam. There are seven fielders behind you that can help you get an out – pitch to contact!

Determining the best pitch to throw should include a quick check of the runners on base and their aggressiveness. Holding runners can be a challenge for most young pitchers. Throws from the set position to a base to hold a runner are often off target. This is mostly seen at first base as a right-hand pitcher's move to first base requires deviation from their normal pitching motion. Means other than throwing to a base can be used to discourage runners from a stealing attempt. For example, varying your 'hold time' will prevent a runner from timing up their break. Long hold times can also cause early runner movement as well as anxiety by the batter. Just stepping back off the rubber can help hold a runner or at least reduce the 'go on first pitcher movement' steal. Head movement can fool some runners. Using different speeds of jump moves can deceive a runner. Throwing to a base before coming to the set position can catch some aggressive runners with big leads. Timing plays with your fielders are best for second and third base pickoffs. All these methods to help hold runners need to be practiced. The mechanism for each needs to be perfected. Failure to practice these will leave a pitcher vulnerable for a balk call or throwing the ball away. As great as it is to pick-off a runner, it is just as bad to let them advance due to an errant base throw.

Determining the best pitch to throw should include your confidence in the called pitch. Is this the best pitch for you in this situation? This batter has a double and homerun off sliders - throw something else? It would be best to get a potential double-play ground ball, but can I consistently throw low fastballs to this batter? I have been throwing the ball past this batter the whole game – let's try for fun a curve ball –NO! Why speed up his bat? Why take the chance of hanging a curve ball? Stick with your best pitch for the situation. Your teammates are counting on you to do just that!

Use specific pitches to setup the following pitch. Pitch sequencing, or the calling of pitch types and locations is an art. Changing a batter's eye level or varying the speed of a pitch can be an effective tool in deceiving the batter. For example, a high fastball followed by a low pitch makes it more difficult for the batter to lock in on a specific location. Alternating inside and outside pitches keeps the batter from crowding the plate or attempting to hit to the opposite field. The changing of speed also is a good deceptive tool for the pitcher. Fastballs followed by changeups are very effective at the high school level. Another setup sequence involves movement variations. A hard slider versus a tailing two seam fastball that moves in the opposite direction can be an effective combination in tricking the batter. Use speed variations, movement directions and location changes to make hitters wonder what is coming next!

Pitching smart means making your best pitch with consideration to the situations presented. Obviously, there is not sufficient time between pitches to go through a thorough analysis to determine what pitch is best to throw. It is experience and knowledge of the game that can allow for rapid pitch determination. Both pitch type and location must be decided. Every pitch is important, and no pitch should be thrown without intent or purpose. Pitches launched nowhere near the strike zone are 'wasted pitches' that serve little purpose, encourage the batter, discourage your fielders, reduce the confidence of the umpire and add to your total pitch count. There is much more to pitching than just throwing the baseball!

Pitching smart includes watching your pitch count. Wasted pitches needlessly increase your pitch totals and contribute to an early exit from the mound. Always try to average 15 pitches per inning. Don't focus on striking every batter out. Pitch to contact and let your fielders make plays. Lots of strikeouts typically drive pitch counts up, while put-outs in the field can greatly reduce the number of pitches thrown in an inning. A one pitch ground ball out is a better out for you than a full count strikeout.

Coaches, pitching smart includes honoring guidelines to protect the health of a pitcher. Keeping track of the number of pitches thrown is key to maintaining the strength and health of a pitcher's arm. Presented below is Table VII-1 suggesting the required days of rest between pitching appearances and the maximum number of pitches to be thrown in a single outing. Recovery time is important, and it is recommended that the guidelines be strictly followed to reduce the likelihood of injury.

Table VII-1: Days of Rest Between Appearances and Maximum Pitches per Outing

Pitcher's Age Bracket	Pitch Count	Days of Rest	Maximum Pitch Count/Outing
10-12 Years Old	< 20 Pitches	None	75 Pitches*
	20-39 Pitches	1 Day	
	40-59 Pitches	2 Days	
	> 60 Pitches	3 Days	
13-15 Years Old	< 25 Pitches	None	95 Pitches*
	25-49 Pitches	1 Day	
	50-69 Pitches	2 Days	
	> 70 Pitches	3 Days	
16-18 Years Old	< 30 Pitches	None	125 Pitches*
	30-49 Pitches	1 Day	
	50-74 Pitches	2 Days	
	> 75 Pitches	3 Days	

*Pitcher may complete pitching to a batter even when maximum count is reached.

Chapter VIII:

Fielding Your Position

Before and after throwing a pitch, pitchers are fielders. To be considered a pitcher and to be held accountable for the rules that govern a pitcher, you must be in contact with the pitching rubber. If you are not in contact with the pitching rubber, you are considered a fielder and not bound by the pitching rules that limit your actions. Many young pitchers understand their immediate fielding responsibilities but fail to execute their defensive assignments after the baseball has been hit past them. Backing up third base and home plate are extremely important assignments and ones that are typically the responsibility of the pitcher. Overthrows are common at both these bases and backing up helps to limit other baserunners from advancing.

After a pitch is thrown pitchers become fielders. Finishing the delivery of a pitch with good mechanics should put pitchers in a position to field balls hit sharply and directly at them. This is one aspect that reinforces the concept of a pitcher keeping their glove out in front near their chest when finishing their pitch. Good mechanics will also leave the pitcher in a balanced position on both feet facing the batter.

Summarized below are the defensive fielding responsibilities of the pitcher and some concepts to help in their execution.

1. **Fielding up the Middle:** Baseballs that are hit near the pitcher, whether a ground ball or a line drive, are potentially easy outs if the pitcher can react fast enough. Finishing a pitch in the proper form will greatly help the pitcher field their position. This requires

landing in a balanced position, not to any one side, and maintaining a glove position in front of their body. It is recommended that part of a pitcher's fielding drills include sharply thrown ground balls, thrown baseballs (line drive simulators) and bunts. These fielding drills should be executed after the pitcher throws a pitch. Both the windup and stretch pitching positions should be used during these fielding drills.

2. **Fielding Bunts:** Most youth and high school teams rely on their pitchers to field most bunts. Only bunts laid down close to the foul lines are not typically fielded by the pitcher. There are two ways to field a bunt that should be practiced by a pitcher. Both methods are dictated by the status of the baseball when the pitcher makes contact.

   a. The rolling bunt should be fielded with the glove and not the bare hand. Foot work is important as the pitcher should try to field the moving bunt with his feet set (aimed) for a throw to a base. Setting the feet is essential to making a good throw. Once the baseball is fielded, it must be transferred to the throwing hand so that a throw can be made. Most off-target throws occur due to improper foot work resulting in imbalance during the throwing motion.

   b. The second way to field a bunt occurs when a bunt is laid down and it stops rolling and is dead on the field. In this case, the pitcher should circle or adjust their path to the ball so as to approach it with their feet in a position to make a throw. When arriving at the baseball, the bare throwing hand pushes down over the top of the ball allowing the fingers to firmly grasp the baseball. With a quick motion, the arm is raised, and the throw is made.

3. **Fielding Ground Balls:** With runners on base, and prior to contacting the pitching rubber, the pitcher should check with the infielders

as to who is covering the base on a steal, on a double play ball or if a runner will be held. In some cases, there may be pre-established conditions that dictate which infielder will be involved. With multiple runners on the bases, it may be unclear as to which base should be thrown to with a come-backer ground ball to the mound. In most cases the lead runner should be focused on, but the game situation should dictate the play. This situation should also be practiced by pitchers to minimize confusion and speedup the opportunity for double plays and lead runner outs.

When ground balls are fielded by the pitcher with no runners on base, the pitcher should always attempt to stride, or if time permits, take a step or two toward first base before making a throw. This action not only shortens the throw and allows the first baseman to get to the base, but it encourages an easy throwing motion, either overhand or underhand. If the pitcher must move toward the third baseline to field the ball, a more rapid and harder throwing action is required.

4. **Covering First Base:** When ground balls are hit to the right side (first base side) of the infield, the pitcher must immediately break toward first base. If the baseball is fielded by the second baseman and the first baseman can get to first base, the pitcher can stop. However, if the first baseman is pulled to his right to field or try to field the ground ball, the pitcher must continue his sprint toward first base to take a potential throw. The pitcher should run straight toward the baseline to a target about 5-7 feet short of first base. Just before he reaches the baseline, he should curve in toward the base and run parallel to the baseline hitting the inside edge of the first base bag with his right foot. If the groundball is fielded, the infielder should throw to the pitcher as soon as possible and prior to the pitcher reaching the bag. An early throw allows the pitcher to focus on catching the throw and then looking

down to see the inside edge of the bag, thus avoiding a collision with the runner. The first baseman may 'call-off' the pitcher from having to cover at any time – the earlier the better!

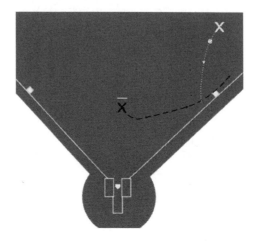

5. **<u>First and Third Defense:</u>** When base runners are on first and third, there is a high likelihood that the runner from first base will either attempt a steal or do a walk-off to distract the pitcher and cause a balk. In that scenario, the pitcher must be aware of the defense as designated by the coach and execute it accordingly. There are multiple options that can be deployed and a signaling system can be used to indicate which defensive strategy is to be employed. The goal in all defensive scenarios will be to try to prevent the runner on third base from scoring. A typical strategy is for the in-fielders to yell 'step off'. The pitcher quickly steps back off the rubber with his pivot foot. If the first base runner is moving or frozen between the bases, the pitcher fires the ball to the second baseman who has been breaking toward the baseline in front of the runner. A tag can be made, or a rundown can ensue. However, at any time that the third base runner makes a move toward home, the catcher yells 'break' and a throw is immediately made to home. *(NOTE: The reason to get the ball as quickly as possible to the second baseman is simply that the pitcher has his back to*

the play which makes recognizing the situation and throwing home more difficult.)

6. **Backing up Bases:** The pitcher is responsible for backing up throws from the outfield to third base and home. Throws to these bases from outfielders or cutoff fielders are frequently off-line, bounce in or are part of a close play. All these situations can result in an overthrow or loose ball that is still in play allowing other runners to advance on the bases. Backing up bases is an important fielding responsibility for the pitcher and should be practiced reinforcing its significance. During team scrimmages or practice drills, include backing up third and home as part of the activity. Include what to look for after fielding an overthrow as runners will be aggressive once they see the loose baseball.

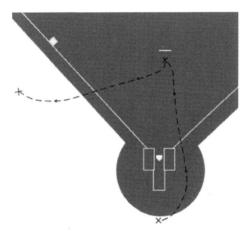

7. **Covering Home Plate - Wild Pitch or Passed Ball:** Whenever a runner is on third base, the pitcher must be able to quickly start toward home plate if there is a wild pitch or passed ball. The pitcher should always be aware of the speed and aggressiveness of the runner on third. This is an indicator of whether a runner will break for home on a wild pitch or passed ball. As a rule, when the pitcher delivers a ball in the dirt, he should always take a step

toward home plate. This action shows that he is ready to defensively cover the plate if necessary. Additionally, this will give him a good start should the pitch get away from the catcher and the runner break from third. If the pitcher needs to cover home plate, he should point to the ball to aid the catcher as he breaks for home plate. Then, he should stop just short of home plate and bend down with his glove facing the catcher, but just up the third base line. The glove location is important as most pitchers stand too tall with their glove up and over the plate. Thus, even with a good throw, the runner can slide under the tag and contact home plate before the glove drops.

8. **Infield fly balls/Foul Line foul balls:** As a pitcher, fly balls in the infield may not be considered their fielding responsibility. This attitude is rooted in professional baseball. However, youth baseball requires the pitcher, often one of the best fielders on the team, to be an active infielder for infield flyballs as well as infield foul balls. Every attempt should be made to field nearby fly balls with an understanding that they may be called off if an infielder can reach the play. Pitchers are fielders after they pitch, and this includes fly balls!

9. **Squeeze Play - Your Responsibility:** When games are tied or close in the late innings, there is a good chance that a runner on third may try to steal home or score using a bunt play (squeeze play). There are several types of squeeze plays, but, if the pitcher is aware of the attempt, there is opportunity to defend the play. First, the pitcher should throw from the stretch position. *(NOTE: It is recommended that with a runner on third the pitcher should always throw from the stretch).* If the third baseman sees the runner break from third, he should yell 'break' to let the pitcher and catcher know that the runner has made an aggressive move toward home. If the batter squares to bunt, the pitcher should

assume a squeeze play. If possible, the pitcher should deliver a high fastball, up out of the strike zone. An alternative pitch would be a low fastball, down out of the zone. The high fastball is a better alternative as it allows the catcher to come out of his crouch to receive the pitch as he will need to dive or move toward the front of the plate. Additionally, if the bunter somehow gets his bat on the ball, it will likely be popped up or fouled back.

This chapter has outlined the many defensive responsibilities of a pitcher with the important concept; A PITCHER BECOMES A FIELDER ONCE THE BASEBALL HAS BEEN PITCHED TO THE PLATE. Perfecting all the defensive responsibilities that a pitcher has is rarely the focus of drills and team practices, but their execution must be practiced. Young pitchers must understand their defensive responsibilities and include them as part of their learning process to become a better pitcher. High school level pitchers should work to perfect their defensive skills and make them a routine part of their game.

Chapter IX:

Holding Runners, Balks

When there is a runner, or runners on base, it is the responsibility of the pitcher to minimize base leads and the stealing of bases. One of the primary tools to accomplish this task is to deliver pitches from the stretch position. By rule, pitchers cannot throw to a base from the windup starting position without first stepping back and off the pitching rubber with their pivot foot. This means that the windup, which is a slower delivery than the stretch, would allow runners to take large leads and have early steal jumps. From the stretch position, throws to the bases are permitted if the pick-off motion follows specific rules. This throwing ability allows the pitcher to hold runners close to their bases. Within the rules there are many actions that can be used by the pitcher to discourage runners from taking long leads and attempting base steals. These measures will be described, and a discussion will be presented covering how they can be employed to slow down the running game of an opposing team.

1) **Understand the Balk Rules:** By definition, a BALK is an illegal movement by the pitcher. All runners are awarded (can advance) one base. An illegal movement is defined by the rules governing the actions of a pitcher. By definition, a player on the field becomes a pitcher whenever their feet contact the pitching rubber. The stance of the pitcher's feet on the pitching rubber defines whether the pitcher is in the windup or stretch throwing position. With runners on base, the pitcher should use the stretch throwing

motion. A balk can only be called by an umpire with runner(s) on base. Some common balk calls are:

a) NOT stepping back off the rubber with your pivot foot <u>first</u> when reverting to a fielder.
b) Not coming to a <u>noticeable</u> pause when pitching from the stretch.
c) When checking runners, moving your shoulders once in the set position.
d) Starting to home plate with the pitch and then throwing to a base.
e) Feinting (faking a throw) to first base without stepping off the rubber first.
f) Dropping the ball while in contact with the pitching rubber.
g) Starting or leaning in to make a pitch but stopping and then restarting.
   NOTE: When a balk is called by an umpire, play is immediately stopped and if a pitch was made it is considered a 'NO PITCH'.

2) **Holding Runners**: When a base runner is attempting to steal a base, they attempt to start their steal move as soon as they think the pitcher is throwing a pitch to the batter. They will first take a lead, in most cases larger than normal, and then make their steal attempt. If they start too early, the pitcher should step back off the pitching rubber with their pivot foot and initiate a play to tag out the runner. If the base stealer is smart, they will start their break as soon as the pitcher commits, by their actions, to make a pitch to the batter. A pitcher can minimize the base runner's break by taking several possible actions. The pitcher's skill to do this is referred to as their ability to 'Hold Runners'. Some of the actions that a pitcher may use to hold baserunners are:

a) Vary their 'HOLD TIME' after coming to a set position.
b) Step back off the pitching rubber with the pivot foot (discourages first move steals).

c) Feint a throw to 2nd or 3rd base if occupied. (A pitcher cannot by rule feint to first base.)

d) <u>Always</u> pitch from the stretch with runners on base.

e) Use different moves when throwing to 1st base.

f) Look at any runners a varying number of times (only moving the head).

g) Throw to a base before or while coming set.

h) Make a throw to a base while straddling the pitching rubber.

i) Pick off a previous runner.

j) Consistently make accurate throws to the bases.

3) **Proficiency of Throws to all Bases**: When making a throw to a base to hold a runner it is important to remember that a bad throw could allow the runner to advance, exactly what you were trying to prevent! Just as throwing mechanics are important to pitching accuracy, the pickoff move to any base must also be performed with proper mechanics. Although the throwing mechanics are less specific, there are a couple of key elements to remember when throwing to an occupied base. The first requirement is that the feet must be positioned properly. This is accomplished with a step, spin, hop or jump of the feet such that they are in line with the targeted base and the foot opposite the throwing arm is in front. Keeping the ball high in the glove prior to the throw speeds up the arm swing back. A short arm or catcher throw is acceptable. Maintaining your shoulders in a level position prevents launching of the baseball. Reaching to the target prevents short hopping the baseball. Throwing over the top and not side arm encourages a straighter and more accurate throw. Practicing your pickoff moves is essential in establishing your personal mechanics and your confidence to make throws when needed.

The list below describes various moves that can be used when throwing to hold or pickoff baserunners.

1. Pickoff Throws to First Base.
    a) Right-Hand Pitchers – (slowest to fastest move)
        I. **Step off Move** – Step back off the pitching rubber with your pivot foot, step toward first base and make your throw. Focus on your target which is the first baseman's glove. This move is slow and more for show. Use it the first time you throw over to first base to deceive the runner that this is your only pickoff move. You can feint a throw to first once you step back off the pitching rubber with your pivot foot.
        NOTE: Just stepping back off the pitching rubber with your pivot foot (with no further action) should cause any runners to return closer to their bases.

        II. **Hop Move with Large Jump** – While in the Set Position, hop with both feet rotating 90 degrees toward first base. Land your feet about 24 inches apart. The stride foot lands out in front and on an imaginary line to first base. The pivot foot ends up about six inches in front of the rubber also on the imaginary line. Drive your throwing arm directly back and point your glove arm toward first base. Keep your shoulders level and make your throw. Focus on your target which is the first baseman's glove and extend your arm toward first base as you release the baseball.

        III. **Hop move with Medium Jump** - While taking the sign and prior to coming set, hop with both feet rotating 90 degrees toward first base. The stride foot lands slightly out in front and on an imaginary line to first base. The pivot foot ends up about 12" to 16" in front of the rubber also on the imaginary line. Drive your throwing arm directly back and point your glove arm toward first base. Keep your shoulders level and make your throw. Focus on your target which is the first baseman's glove and extend your arm toward first base as you release the baseball.

IV. **Hop move with Small Jump** - While in the Set Position, hop with both feet rotating 90 degrees toward first base. Keep the hop quick and the feet relatively close to each other. The stride foot lands slightly out in front and on an imaginary line to first base. The pivot foot ends up directly in front of the rubber also on the imaginary line. Drive your throwing arm directly back and point your glove arm toward first base. Keep your shoulders level and make your throw. Focus on your target which is the first baseman's glove and extend your arm toward first base as you release the baseball.

b) Left-Hand Pitchers

I. **Step Back and Throw** – While in the set position, start your arm back while stepping back off the pitching rubber with your pivot foot. Your stride foot remains in place about 12" to 16" in front of the rubber. Try to keep your body from moving while you take your arm back behind you. Keep your glove arm in the same set position. Throw over to first extending your arm toward first base as you throw. Since your feet are not moving and are perpendicular to first base, this throwing motion is pretty much 100% arm. Keep your shoulders level and make your throw. Focus on your target which is the first baseman's glove.

NOTE: Using this step back move, you are allowed by rule to feint a throw to first. *This is the only time a pitcher can fake a throw to first base.*

II. **Stride Leg Lift and Throw:** While in the set position, lift the stride leg up and drop it down but step toward first base and make your throw. Timing of both arm actions is like that of a normal pitch. As the stride foot starts down, the throwing arm is taken back, and the glove arm is taken forward pointing to first base. When the stride foot lands, the throwing arm should be starting forward. Keep your shoulders level and make your throw. Focus on your target which is the first baseman's glove.

III. **Stride Leg Slide and Throw:** While in the set position, lift the stride leg slightly and drive it in a slide step action toward first base and make your throw. Timing of both arm actions is like that of a normal pitch. As the stride foot slides forward, the throwing arm is taken back, and the glove arm is taken forward pointing to first base. When the stride foot lands, the throwing arm should be starting forward. Keep your shoulders level and make your throw. Focus on your target which is the first baseman's glove.

NOTE: Just stepping back off the pitching rubber with your pivot foot (with no further action) should cause any runners to return closer to their bases.

2. Pick-off Throws to Second Base

a) Right-Hand Pitchers – Since runners are not typically held at second base, throws to the base should be in conjunction with either the second baseman or shortstop breaking to the bag. This can be accomplished by a set timing play or just positioning one of the infielders close to the base.

I. **Hop Move with Throw or Feint:** While in the set position, make a hop move rotating your body to the glove side 180 degrees. On landing, your feet should be on an imaginary line running toward second base, your stride foot in front. As you execute your hopping rotation, start to extend both arms, your glove arm toward second base and your pitching arm back toward home plate getting loaded to throw. Upon landing, you can throw, feint a throw, or charge the runner. The actual choice is a function of what the base runner is doing. Keep your shoulders level when you make a throw.

II. **Spin Move with Throw or Feint:** While in the set position, lift your stride leg to 90 degrees and pivot with a spinning motion back and around to the right. As you spin, start to extend both arms, your glove arm toward second base and your pitching arm back toward home plate getting loaded to throw. When you face second base, you can drop your stride foot. Upon landing, you can throw, feint a throw, or charge the runner. The actual choice is a function of what the base runner is doing. Keep your shoulders level if you make a throw.

III. **Step Back with Throw or Feint:** While in the set position, step back off the pitching rubber with your pivot foot. Your stride foot remains in place while you step back with your pivot foot to behind the rubber. Keep your glove arm in the same set position. Now you can step toward second with your stride foot turning right or left, whichever seems more natural to you. Basically, when you step, you will step past your pivot foot, so your stride foot is now in front of you as you face second base. As you step with your stride foot, start to extend both arms, your glove arm toward second base and your pitching arm back toward home plate getting loaded to throw. Upon landing, you can throw, feint a throw, or charge the runner. The actual choice is a function of what the base runner is doing. Keep your shoulders level if you make a throw.

b) Left-Hand Pitchers - Since runners are not typically held at second base, throws to the base should be in conjunction with either the second baseman or shortstop breaking to the bag. This can be accomplished by a set timing play or just positioning one of the infielders close to the base.

    I.   **Hop Move with Throw or Feint:** While in the set position, make a hop move rotating your body to the glove side 180 degrees. On landing, your feet should be on an imaginary line running toward second base, your stride foot in front. As you execute your hopping rotation, start to extend both arms, your glove arm toward second base and your pitching arm back toward home plate getting loaded to throw. Upon landing, you can throw, feint a throw, or charge the runner. The actual choice is a function of what the base runner is doing. Keep your shoulders level when you make a throw.

    II.   **Spin Move with Throw or Feint:** While in the set position, lift your stride leg to 90 degrees and pivot with a spinning motion back and around to the left. As you spin, start to extend both arms, your glove arm toward second base and your pitching arm back toward home plate getting loaded to throw. When you face second base, you can drop your stride foot. Upon landing, you can throw, feint a throw, or charge the runner. The actual choice is a function of what the base runner is doing. Keep your shoulders level if you make a throw.

    III.   **Step Back with Throw or Feint:** While in the set position, step back off the pitching rubber with your pivot foot. Your stride foot remains in place while you step back with your pivot foot to behind the rubber. Keep your glove arm in the same set position. Now you can step toward second with your stride foot turning right or left, whichever seems more natural to you. Basically, when you step, you will step past your pivot foot, so your stride foot is now in front of you as you face second base. As you step with your stride foot, start to extend both arms, your glove arm toward second base and your pitching arm back toward home plate getting loaded to throw. Upon landing, you can throw, feint a throw, or charge the runner. The actual choice is a function of what the base runner is doing. Keep your shoulders level if you make a throw.

3. Pick-off Throws to Third Base

    a) Right-Hand Pitchers – Since runners are not typically held at third base, throws to the base should be in conjunction with the third baseman breaking to the bag. This can be accomplished by a set timing play or just positioning the third baseman close to the base.

        I. **Step Back and Throw** – While in the set position, step back off the pitching rubber with your pivot foot. As you step back, start taking your throwing arm back to load. Your stride foot remains in place about 12" to 16" in front of the rubber. Try to keep your body from moving while you take your arm back behind you. Keep your glove arm in the same set position. Throw over or feint to third base extending your arm toward third as you throw. Since your feet are not moving and are perpendicular to third base, this throwing motion is pretty much 100% arm. Keep your shoulders level and make your throw. Focus on your target which is the third baseman's glove.

        II. **Stride Leg Lift and Throw:** While in the set position, lift the stride leg up and drop it down but step directly toward third base and make your throw. Timing of both arm actions is like that of a normal pitch. As the stride foot starts down, the throwing arm is taken back, and the glove arm is taken forward pointing to third base. When the stride foot lands, the throwing arm should be starting forward. Keep your shoulders level and make your throw. Focus on your target which is the third baseman's glove.

III. **Stride Leg Slide and Throw:** While in the set position, lift the stride leg slightly and drive it in a slide step action toward third base and make your throw. Timing of both arm actions is like that of a normal pitch. As the stride foot slides forward, the throwing arm is taken back, and the glove arm is taken forward pointing to third base. When the stride foot lands, the throwing arm should be starting forward. Keep your shoulders level and make your throw. Focus on your target which is the third baseman's glove.

NOTE: Just stepping back off the pitching rubber with your pivot foot (with no further action) should cause any runners to return closer to their bases.

b) Left-Hand Pitchers - Since runners are not typically held at third base, throws to the base should be in conjunction with the third baseman breaking to the bag. This can be accomplished by a set timing play or just positioning the third baseman close to the base.

I. **Step off Move** – Step back off the pitching rubber with your pivot foot, step toward third base and make your throw. Focus on your target which is the third baseman's glove. This move is slow and more for show. Use it the first time you throw over to third base to deceive the runner that this is your only pick-off move. You can feint a throw to third once you step back off the pitching rubber with your pivot foot.

NOTE: Just stepping back off the pitching rubber with your pivot foot (with no further action) should cause any runners to return closer to their bases.

II. **Hop Move with Large Jump** – While in the set position, hop with both feet rotating 90 degrees toward third base. Land your feet about 24 inches apart. The stride foot lands out in front and on an imaginary line to third base. The pivot foot ends up about a foot in front of the rubber also on the imaginary line. Drive your throwing arm directly back and point your glove arm toward third base. Keep your shoulders level and make your throw. Focus on your target which is the third baseman's glove.

III. **Hop move with Medium Jump** - While taking the sign and prior to coming set, hop with both feet rotating 90 degrees toward third base. The stride foot lands slightly out in front and on an imaginary line to third base. The pivot foot ends up about 12" to 16" in front of the rubber also on the imaginary line. Drive your throwing arm directly back and point your glove arm toward third base. Keep your shoulders level and make your throw. Focus on your target which is the third baseman's glove.

IV. **Hop move with Small Jump** - While in the set position, hop with both feet rotating 90 degrees toward third base. Keep the hop quick and the feet relatively close to each other. The stride foot lands slightly out in front and on an imaginary line to third base. The pivot foot ends up directly in front of the rubber also on the imaginary line. Drive your throwing arm directly back and point your glove arm toward third base. Keep your shoulders level and make your throw.

Focus on your target which is the third baseman's glove.

Stepping back off the rubber is an excellent way to slow down your opponent's running game. However, the step off move is also a good safety measure for the following situations:

1) If a pitch is not to be made (for any reason), to prevent a balk call once your pivot foot has been placed on or against the rubber, always <u>step back off the rubber</u> with your pivot foot.
2) Step off if any fielder or coach yells 'Step-Off'.
3) Step off if you do not feel right, or you just want to reset your thoughts.
4) Step off if you want to see if any runners are going on first movement.
5) Step off if you hear someone yell 'time'.
6) Step off if any of the umpires are not ready.
7) Step off if the wind blows dirt at you or your infielders.

Varying your hold time is an important tool for discouraging base stealing. When holding runners on base, always vary your hold time from pitch to pitch so that runners cannot anticipate your pitch to home plate. When making moves to any base, use different move speeds to confuse the runners. Using varying head movements or looks to a base are helpful. Make sure that you use all your tools to help you as a pitcher hold base runners and reduce steal attempts.

Chapter X:

Staying Physically Strong

Routines are important in standardizing both your physical and mental preparation for a successful pitching season. An off-season conditioning program is strongly recommended. It can be used to strengthen muscle groups and improve explosive actions. Also, it is strongly suggested that whenever you pitch, you establish a pregame and postgame routine. The pregame program should be structured to prepare your body for the rigorous pitching motions required. The postgame routine should help you recover more quickly and minimize the potential for injury. Sample pregame (warm-up routine) and postgame routines are listed below.

Pregame Warm-up Routine

1) Starters
   a. Stretching for 7-10 minutes (upper and lower body).
   b. Start tossing at 30 feet with a partner – step back 2 to 5 steps after each throw until reaching 100 feet. Throws should be on a line and at the receiver's chest.
   c. Toss 3-5 throws on the bull-pen mound (55 feet), then begin throwing from the wind-up.
   d. Throw each of your pitches 3-4 times from the wind-up.
   e. Throw each of your pitches 3-4 times from the stretch.
   f. From the stretch, throw 2 complete sequences of all your pitch types.
   g. Finish with three high 4-seam fastballs.

2) Relievers (obviously this is time dependent)
   a. Stretching for 3-5 minutes (mainly arm).
   b. Start tossing at 30 feet – stepping back (2 to 5 steps) after each throw until reaching 100 feet. (skip this step if time is short)
   c. Toss 5-8 throws on the bull-pen mound (55 feet), then begin throwing from the wind-up.
   d. Throw each of your pitches 2 times from the wind-up.
   e. Throw each of your pitches 3-5 times from the stretch.
   f. From the stretch, throw 1 sequence of all pitch types.
   g. Finish with three high 4-seam fastballs.

It is typical for pitchers to suffer shoulder or elbow soreness after their outing. Common places to sense discomfort are in the biceps near the elbow or shoulder, in the triceps near the elbow, and in the shoulder rotator cuff. Strengthening exercises can help reduce injuries to these areas but soreness from extensive explosive use is difficult to prevent. Post-game routines are geared toward removing lactic acid from your muscles and increasing the supply of nutrients required for muscles to recover from stress. Icing helps reduce inflammation and can be used as well. It is recommended that arm soreness should be addressed and not ignored as further stress on aching muscles can lead to a more extensive injury. Below is a sample post game routine that can be used for pitchers. Also included is some information regarding icing.

Post-Game Cool-Down Routine

1) Running Poles – After the game, jog from 3rd base (or 1st base) to the left field foul pole (or right field foul pole) and back to the base – this is considered to be 'ONE POLE'.
2) Follow the recommendations below for the Number of Poles to Jog:
   a. For 2 innings or less – run 1 pole.
   b. For 2 to 4 innings – run 2 poles.
   c. For more than 4 innings – run 3 poles.

Icing and Stretching

1) Ice any tender, sore or tight arm or shoulder areas for 15-20 minutes.
2) Icing can be performed any time after the game - the sooner the better!
3) The following morning stretch your arm and any sore areas.
4) Heat can be used to reduce stiffness and improve nutrient replenishment.
5) Continue evening icing and morning stretching daily if soreness lingers.
6) DO NOT ice if you plan to throw again soon. For example, if after pitching for several innings you go play a position in the field.

Obviously, injury is a threat to all athletes. Although rest is a great healer once an injury occurs, the time for recovery removes the athlete from competition. There are preventive measures that can help minimize the potential threat of arm problems. Most pitching injuries are arm related and can be minimized by off season strengthening exercises. The workouts should be designed based on the equipment and space available. A pre-season conditioning program for pitchers should include conditioning in the following areas.

Pre-season Conditioning Groups for Pitchers:

1) Upper Body Exercises
2) Rotator Cuff Exercises
3) Lower Body Exercises
4) Arm Explosion Exercises
5) General Agility Exercises
6) Core Strengthening Exercises

There are many different exercises that can be used to strengthen each of the above areas. The Internet is a great source for videos that focus on specific muscle groups. It is important not to limit your exercise program due to lack of time, equipment, or space. There are many options and work arounds that will always permit you to have an off- season workout program. Taking care of your body is important for any athlete.

Example of Pre-Season Conditioning Exercises
for the Upper Body Including Rotator Cuff Exercises

This is a 20–25-minute workout that should be repeated 2 to 3 times per week.

Band Exercises (choose a band that matches your strength limitations)

1. **Bicep Curls – Palms Up (10-15 reps):** Place band under your feet. Hold your band in each hand with your palms facing up. Start with both arms at your side, pull hands up to your chest keeping elbows tight to your side. Return slowly.

2. **Bicep Curls – Palms Down (10-15 reps):** Place band under your feet. Hold your band in each hand with your palms facing down. Start with both arms at your side, pull hands up to your chest keeping elbows tight to your side. Return slowly.

3. **Bicep Curls – Palms Facing Each Other (10-15 reps):** Place band under your feet. Hold your band in each hand with your palms facing each other. Start with both arms at your side, pull hands up to your chest keeping elbows tight to your side. Return slowly.

4. **Pull Aparts – Shoulder Front (10-15 reps):** Grip band in front of you with both hands about 16-24" apart, arms fully extended out in front of you at shoulder height. Pull your arms apart as far as you can. Control the return.

5. **Pull Aparts – Shoulder Back (10-15 reps):** Grip band in front of you with both hands about 6-10" apart, arms at shoulder height, hands against your chest with elbows bent. Keep your elbows up and pull your hands apart as far as you can. Control the return.

6. **Pull Aparts – Elbows (10-15 reps):** Grip band in front of you with both hands about 6-10" apart, arms down at your side but elbows bent with lower arms extending straight out in front of you. Keep

both elbows at your side and pull your hands apart as far as you can. Control the return.

7. **Side Arm Lifts (10 reps):** Place band under your feet. Hold your band in each hand with your palms facing down. Start with both arms at your side, lift your arms up and to the side on each side as far as you can while keeping your arms straight. Control going back down with both arms returning to your side.

8. **Front Arm Lifts (10 reps):** Place band under your feet. Hold your band in each hand with your palms facing down. Start with both arms at your side, lift your arms up in front of you as far as you can while keeping your arms straight. Control going back down with both arms returning to your side.

9. **Single Arm Press Upward (10 reps each arm):** Place band under your feet. Hold your band in each hand with more band on your right side. Start with your right arm at your side with a bent elbow and your forearm pointing straight up. Lift your hand and arm straight up as high as you can. Control returning to your starting position. Adjust your band and repeat with your left arm.

10. **Modified Row Pull (10-15 reps):** Fasten your band to a secure point such that two ends come out from the tie-off point. Face the bands and grab each end with one of your hands. Step back putting tension on the bands and let your arms extend toward the bands. Arch your back and pull both bands toward you. Keep your hands together as you pull your hands into your chest. Your elbows should bend out as you pull the bands into your chest. Control your return as your arms move back to the starting position.

11. **Modified Skull Crushers (10-15 reps):** Fasten your band to a secure point such that two ends come out from the tie-off point. Turn your back to the bands and grab each end with one of your hands. Locate the bands above your head. Step forward putting tension on the bands. Your elbows should be bent above your head with your forearms stretched by the bands back behind you. Arch your back and pull both bands forward over your head while

keeping your elbows at a fixed point above your head. Keep your hands together as you pull your hands forward. Your elbows should bend as you pull the bands from behind you to in front of you. Control your return as your arms move back to the starting position.

12. **Push Outs (10-15 reps):** Fasten your band to a secure point such that two ends come out from the tie-off point. Turn your back to the bands and grab each end with one of your hands. Locate the bands to each side of you. Your arms should be at your sides with the elbows bent and the forearms pointing up. Step forward to put tension on the bands. Start by extending both arms out from your body. Push straight out and back in a controlled fashion.

13. **Elbow Pulls at Shoulder Height (10 reps and 15 seconds of explosion):** Fasten your band such that two ends come out from a secure tie-off point. Extend your throwing arm straight back and out from your side pointing back toward the tie-off point. Grab both ends of the band with your throwing hand and rotate your forearm from your elbow straight up. At this point your upper arm is extending out from your shoulder at 90 degrees and your forearm is pointing up and at 90 degrees to your upper arm. Step forward so that the bands are in tension and pull your forearm back and down. Begin the exercise by pulling your hand and forearm forward while keeping your elbow at a fixed position. Your hand and forearm should rotate around your elbow as you pull the band forward. Control both the pull and return. Try to keep the elbow at a fixed position. Immediately after ten reps, begin a 15 second period of rapid arm drive exploding as you start your arm forward.

14. **Elbow Pulls at Waist Height (10 reps and 15 seconds of explosion):** Fasten your band such that two ends come out from the secure tie-off point. At your waist, extend your throwing forearm straight out from your side. Grab both ends of the band with your throwing hand. At this point your upper arm is at your side and your forearm is pointing out to the side at 90 degrees from your

waist. Step forward so that the bands are in tension and pull your forearm back. Begin the exercise by pulling your hand and forearm forward and into your waist while keeping your elbow at a fixed position against your side. Your hand and forearm should rotate around your elbow as you pull the band forward. Control both the pull and return. Try to keep the elbow at a fixed position. Immediately after ten reps, begin a 15 second period of rapid arm drive exploding as you start your arm forward.

Similar exercises can be used for core and lower body development. Bands, which are more easily obtained at a reasonable cost can be used instead of weights. Note that exercises with bands are less likely to cause injury. The use of bands also allows for strength improvement as well as muscle explosiveness, both important factors for throwing with more velocity and hitting with more power.

NOTE: If outside facilities are available for off season workouts, long toss is a great way to increase arm strength. Consult the Internet to see videos on the proper mechanisms for long toss.

Chapter XI:

Drills for Pitchers

When practice time is available, there are many drills that can be used to assist in the improvement of pitching shortcomings. These include drills to aid in advancing proper pitching mechanics, fielding assignments and base pickoff moves. Because baseball is a fast reaction sport, muscle memory is important in executing most movements on the field. Pitching is a very repetitive action that relies on muscle memory to deliver pitches using consistent mechanics. To change a pitcher's motion, their muscle memory must be altered. This requires repetitive drills that simulate proper form. Listed below are some routine pitching problems and drills that can help correct them. Note that the drills need to be repeated many times over as improvement will only come when muscle memory accepts the new form.

1. **Drills for Issues with Pitching Mechanics:**
    Problem Description: The windup starting step is too large or in the wrong direction causing significant head and body movement during the initial phase of the windup pitching motion.

    Drill to Correct: Start with the proper windup stance, either on a simulated pitching rubber or on an actual mound. Repetitively take your weight shift step to a marked position and minimize head and body movement. Eyes should be constantly on the target. Repeat the stepping motion at least 25 times.

Problem Description: While in the windup, the pivot foot is placed on top of the rubber, or not in contact with the front edge of the pitching rubber.

Drill to Correct: Start with the proper windup stance, either on a simulated pitching rubber or on an actual mound. Repetitively take your weight shift step and lift and locate your pivot foot against the front edge of the pitching rubber. Repeat the pivot foot locating motion at least 25 times. Achieve a point when you do not need to look down to place your pivot foot properly. Your eyes should always stay focused on your target.

Problem Description: While throwing from the windup, your leg lift is inconsistent and does not come to the same point with each pitch. *The goal is to lift it to 90 degrees consistently since this stopping point is easy to distinguish.*

Drill to Correct: Stand with your back to a wall. Place your glove hand just under your chin with a baseball in your throwing hand. Feet should be 8 to 12 inches apart and pointing out from the wall. Lift what will be your stride foot up to a point where your thigh is parallel to the ground (90-degrees out from your body). Your foot should be loose and hang down. When you reach the 90-degree lift location, drop your leg straight down to a point 2-3 inches from the floor. Continue to repeat the leg lift and drop process 25 times.

Problem Description: While throwing from the windup, you start your stride-out before your leg lift drops to 2-3 inches above the mound. *This is a falling motion rather than an accelerated push off the rubber. It also results in a hard landing with your stride foot.*

Drill to Correct: Stand with your back to a wall. Place your glove hand just under your chin with a baseball in your throwing hand. Feet should be 8 to 12 inches apart and pointing out from the wall. Lift what will be your stride foot up to a point where your thigh is parallel to the ground (90-degrees out from your body). Your foot should be loose and hang down. When you reach the 90-degree lift location, drop your leg straight down to a point 2-3 inches from the floor and drive your stride leg forward. Repeat the leg lift, drop, and stride process 20 times.

Problem Description: When you land with your stride foot, it is not in line with your target or is either too far open or closed.

Drill to Correct: Create a line about 6-8 feet long running perpendicular from the center of the mound toward home plate. If inside use tape or other floor markings. Go through your windup start and stride out attempting to land on the created line. Your stride foot should land pointing at your target or slightly closed with respect to your target. If open (rotated past the line), your hips are over rotating. Repeat until 10 consecutive windup strides are correct.

Problem Description: Your stride foot does not extend out far enough from the pitching rubber. You fall off to the stride foot side at the end of your delivery.

Drill to Correct: A towel drill is ideal to correct falling off issues and improve drive from the pitching rubber during the stride. Obtain a small towel (like a dish towel). Place the towel in your throwing hand between your fingers such that the towel is split in half. Have a player stand about 6-8 feet in front of you holding their glove out in front of them at waist height. Start your windup and stride toward the player. Drive your throwing arm and snap the towel down attempting to hit the players extended glove. Once you hit the glove, have the player move back 2-4 inches and repeat your throwing motion. Have the player move back whenever you can consistently strike the glove with your arm snapping motion. Try to extend your stride step and drive out with an aggressive motion. Repeat the drill focusing on improving your stride length and foot landing position.

Problem Description: Pitches miss their target left or right due to shoulder rotation when the baseball is taken back. The back shoulder rotates slightly behind the target line causing the front shoulder to point off the target line.

Drill to Correct: An arm swing drill can help with this problem. Stand with your back to a wall. Hold your hands in a starting pitch position just under your chin. Step forward along the wall with your stride foot. As you take your stride step, swing both arms. Your glove arm goes forward along the wall and your throwing hand backwards along the wall. When you take the ball back with your throwing arm, try not to hit the wall with any part of your throwing arm. Keep both your shoulders close to the wall as you swing both arms. Do not turn or rotate your shoulders as you take the ball back. This forces you to take the ball straight back and not to the side behind you as your arm will hit the wall. Repeat 25 times or until you can consistently not touch the wall with either arm/hand as you swing both arms.

Problem Description: Having trouble with the height of pitches is most likely due to being unable to consistently take the baseball back to the same take-back position. *The take-back position is the maximum arm extension point at which the arm stops moving back and begins to move forward. Since this occurs during the backward arm swing it is a point on the arm's swing arc where direction of the baseball changes.*

Drill to Correct: Ideally you should take the ball back to the same take-back spot with every pitch. A large sweeping throwing arm motion makes it difficult to constantly hit the same take-back spot. A varying and inconsistent take-back spot will cause pitches to miss high or low. By simplifying the arm swing you can improve the likelihood of hitting the same take-back spot. Stand with your back to a wall. Place both hands just under your chin with a baseball in your throwing hand. Feet should be 8 to 12 inches apart and pointing out from the wall. Together, drive both elbows straight out to each side and up. Separate your hands and swing them downward and then out as your elbows drive to shoulder height. Your hands should not swing below your waist. Drive your elbows to shoulder height while swinging your hands to shoulder height or above. The throwing hand will track to a consistent take-back location. Your glove hand will swing in front of you and point at your target. Make sure you swing your arms straight back keeping them close to your body as they swing past your chest. Staying close to your body helps to maintain a straight take away. Repeat 25 times.

Problem Description: A pitcher having trouble bending at the waist and getting out over their stride foot will tend to fall to a side as they finish their delivery.

Drill to Correct: You need a partner spaced about 15-20 feet in front of you. Both of you should get down on one knee, the knee on your throwing arm side is down. Place your glove hand just under your chin with a baseball in your throwing hand. Swing your arms (properly) and stop at full arm extension. Now throw the baseball to your partner and after release continue your arm motion and touch the ground in front of you. Bend at the waist and reach out as far as you can. Your target should be the chest of your partner. As you throw, also bring your glove hand and chest together. Repeat this drill 20 times.

Problem Description: A pitcher that throws across their body will miss left and right. This is a sign of throwing too much side-arm!

Drill to Correct: You need a partner spaced about 20-25 feet in front of you. Place your glove hand just under your chin with a baseball in your throwing hand. Swing your arms (properly) and stop at full arm extension. Now, take a step forward and throw the baseball to your partner and after release continue your arm motion and touch your glove side knee. When you throw, bend at the waist, and reach out as far as you can. Your target should be the chest of your partner. As you throw, also bring your glove and chest together. If you finish across your chest or waist, you are throwing side-arm. Repeat the finishing drill 20 times.

Problem Description: As I finish my throwing motion, my pivot foot drags behind but eventually comes to rest across from my stride foot. *Your pivot foot leg should be driven from the pitching rubber 'up and over' as you follow through with your pitch. If it drags, you are not getting enough drive as you stride forward, or your hip rotation is not contributing much to your pitching motion.*

Drill to Correct: Place a bucket halfway down your stride length but on the side of your trailing leg. Go through your pitching motion and when you pull your back foot forward, accelerate your hips and pull your pivot leg over the bucket. Also, try pushing off the rubber with an initial explosion forward. Your pivot foot should still land out in front at the same distance as your stride foot. Once you land your body should be balanced and not fall to a side or forward. If you correct your foot dragging and still fall to a side, most likely the falling is an indication of an issue with your stride foot. Check for stride foot location and direction upon landing. Repeat 10-15 times getting a feel for driving your hip and pulling the leg over the bucket.

2. **Drills for Issues with Pitcher Fielding Responsibilities:**

    Problem Description: Whenever the pitcher fields a bunt that has stopped, they look up and mishandle the baseball. It never gets in their hand so a throw can be made. *If a hit or bunted baseball has stopped rolling, place your hand on top of the ball and push down to get a good grip. Do not try to pick it up by grabbing it or scooping with your glove.*

    Drill to Correct: Place 8-10 baseballs randomly in front of home plate. Have the pitcher come off the mound and properly grab one of the baseballs (pushing down) and make a throw to first base. Start with balls closer to first and move to balls further away. This drill can also help with foot work. Have the pitcher try to align their feet toward first base as they pick up the baseballs.

    Problem Description: Pitcher fails to cover first base on a baseball hit to the right side. *Pitchers should always take an immediate step toward first base anytime the baseball is hit on the ground to their left side.*

    Drill to Correct: With a pitcher on the mound, a simulated pitch is made. A ground ball is hit by a coach to the right side of the infield. The pitcher must take a step toward first and break if appropriate to cover first base.

Problem Description: The pitcher never moves or takes the proper route to cover first base when ground balls are hit to the right side of the infield.

Drill to Correct: With a pitcher on the mound, a simulated pitch is made. A ground ball is hit by a coach to the right side of the infield. The pitcher must take a step toward first and break if appropriate to first base. The path should be toward the baseline at a spot short of first base, and then up the inside of the baseline to the base. Any throw by the fielder to the pitcher should be before the pitcher reaches the base. This allows the pitcher to locate first base and time their last step for contact on the inside of the bag by the right foot.

Problem Description: The pitcher has difficulty throwing accurately to a base after fielding a ground ball or bunt.

Drill to Correct: With runners on base and a pitcher on the mound, a simulated pitch is made. A ground ball is hit by a coach toward the pitcher. The pitcher must determine which base to throw to. Try this drill with runners on first, and runners on first and second. Repeat with bunts rather than ground balls. Have the catcher yell which base to throw to depending on the bunt's location and speed.

Problem Description: The pitcher fails to cover home plate with a runner on third and a passed ball or wild pitch occurs.

Drill to Correct: With a pitcher on the mound and a catcher behind home plate, a simulated pitch is made. A coach rolls a ball behind the catcher to the left, right, or directly behind. The pitcher must point to the ball yelling "ball, ball" and break towards home plate. Upon arriving the pitcher faces the catcher and holds their glove about a foot above the base and 12 to 24 "up the third base line.

As soon as a throw is made and caught, the pitcher drives their glove down and slightly up the third base line to make the tag. The pitcher's feet should be inside the foul-line just in front of home plate.

Problem Description: The pitcher has problems picking up high fly balls near the mound or foul lines.

Drill to Correct: With a pitcher on the mound, a simulated pitch is made. A fly ball is hit high in the air, (preferably with backspin) such that it lands in an area that the pitcher can reach. If other fielders are present, practice who has priority calling for the fly ball.

Problem Description: The pitcher has problems remembering to back-up third base and home plate on relay throws from the outfield.

Drill to Correct: With a pitcher on the mound and fielders at all positions, hit gap shots to the outfield. Place runners at all bases and instruct the pitcher to back up either third base or home depending on the situation that occurs in the field. Repeat for different scenarios until the pitcher understands where to back-up the play.

3. **Drills for Issues with Pick-off Throws to the Bases:**
   Problem Description: The pitcher's moves and throws to first base to hold runners are erratic with poor throw location.

   Drill to Correct: Either on a baseball field or simulated field, have the pitcher work on various moves to first base. Each move should be scrutinized for correct form and speed of execution. Throws to first base should not be included until the pitcher has demonstrated proper foot work and arm movements for each move.

Once the physical aspects of each move have been confirmed, throws to first base can be added to each pick-off attempt. Throws should be to a target (first baseman's glove) and be consistent through the various move types.

Problem Description: The pitcher's moves and tosses to second base to hold runners are erratic with poor throw location.

Drill to Correct: Either on a baseball field or simulated field, have the pitcher work on various moves to second base. Each move should be scrutinized for correct form and speed of execution. Throws to second base should not be included until the pitcher has demonstrated proper foot work and arm actions for each move. Once the physical aspects of each move have been confirmed, throws to second can be added to each pick-off attempt. Throws should be to a target (second base) and be consistent through the various move types. A runner can be used to add additional complexity to the drill. This can reinforce the concept of an accurate throw as tags will have to be made and it will be obvious that an inaccurate throw will slow the speed of a tag.

Problem Description: The pitcher's moves and tosses to third base to hold runners are erratic with poor throw location.

Drill to Correct: Either on a baseball field or simulated field, have the pitcher work on various moves to third base. Each move should be scrutinized for correct form and speed of execution. Throws to third base should not be included until the pitcher has demonstrated proper foot work and arm actions for each move. Once the physical aspects of each move have been confirmed, throws to third can be added to each pick-off attempt. Throws should be to a target (third baseman) and be consistent through the various move types. A runner can be used to demonstrate the importance of the accuracy of the throw as a run will score if the ball gets by the third baseman.

Problem Description: With runners on base, the pitcher does not step back off the rubber and commits a balk whenever an unfamiliar or unusual situation occurs.

Drill to Correct: Either on a baseball field or simulated field, have the pitcher work on what to do when a fielder or coach yells 'step-off'. Create different scenarios with base runners. Have the runners break at different times while a pitcher is on the mound. Infielders should yell 'step-off'. The pitcher should step-off the rubber with their pivot foot and turn immediately to face the lead runner. At that time, the pitcher should initiate a throw or another action to counteract the runner's attempt to steal. Repetitive drills are important to combat aggressive base runners as pitcher's can be easily distracted by their actions causing wild base throws and even wild pitches.

Problem Description: Executing the defense for special offensive plays. *Most offensive plays occur when the game is close, and the opponent is trying to advance runners or score a run. Plays are usually designed to create confusion or deception and practicing a defensive strategy is important for a successful defense. In most situations, plays occur while the pitcher has the baseball.*

Drill to Correct: Defensive drills should be designed and practiced for special situations such as the squeeze play or the first and third steal play. Drills enacting each unique offensive play should be designed and practiced helping the pitcher recognize the situation and how to react.